BOTTLED WOUNDS

Mike Lawson

AUTHORED BY:
Mike Lawson

EDITED BY:
Tobyn Lawson

COVER ART BY:
Kerry Clavadetscher

CHAPTER ART BY:
Maggie Ronan

PRINTED BY LULU PRESS INC.
Printed in the United States of America
Available in paperback and e-book from Lulu and other major online retail outlets

First Printing Edition, 2021
ISBN 978-1-6671-5996-6

Book formatting template: Free download by https://usedtotech.com

To find out more about the author, visit Coachmiketraining.com

DEDICATION

I dedicate this book to my wife and two sons, who have endured my dysfunctional behavior while I did the personal work to heal my wounded soul and become a better husband, father and man.

For them, I am truly grateful.

I would also like to honor The Mankind Project for gifting me the tools to fix my broken heart.

I salute you.

CONTENTS

Prologue

In my childhood years, my parents gifted me with many emotional demons. These dark shadows hid within my heart for many years. Now at 52 years old, and following over 20 years of deep, painful personal work, I feel that I have conquered my monsters and healed my festering wounds that lived within my soul. I have come to realize that fighting the darkest beasts within me was much more painful than battling anything that existed in the physical world.

Over the years, I have listened to countless experiences and stories from different sources, whether it be coworkers, friends or documentaries. In most instances, people have one or two horrific things that they experienced in their childhood days which later in life sent them down a dysfunctional path of personal destruction. This is a wide path with plenty of room for variance. Some turn to alcohol or drugs, while others turn to abuse and violence. The element of self-destruction is also key, ranging from eating disorders to suicidal tendencies. The various combinations of these negative addictions and behaviors is what makes them so hard to unpack and deal with. I am not writing this book to say that I have had it worse than anybody else. After watching hundreds of men like myself that have decided to do their deepest, darkest work to get rid of the demons within their soul, I have come to what I deem to be a key realization: there is no weighing our demons. Our wounds, whether we judge them as minor or major, impact all of our emotions differently. There is no sense in competing for supremacy of victimhood, as this energy is better spent addressing one's personal traumas and helping others to overcome theirs.

Once you acquire these monsters, the quest to confront them is fierce. It requires you to peel off layers of yourself until you find the infestation within your heart. For me, this was the most intense battle I have ever been in. The hardest part of my own personal work was owning my stuff, the things that I was hiding from everybody in my world. The truths that I did not want people to know about me and my shadows that I suppressed. In this book, I will tell you short stories of how I acquired these many demons as a child. I will detail how I confronted them early in my life to survive and years later, how I decided to confront each emotional wound the demons had left in order to make peace possible in my heart. I can honestly say that before I started this journey to being a healthy person, the sight of my reflection in the mirror only induced extreme negativity.

"I hate myself"

"I don't trust myself"

"I don't forgive myself"

"I am not worthy for happiness"

"Anger is the solution always"

"I don't deserve to live"

"I hate God for putting me through this"

"Hate is my ally"

"Violence is always the solution"

"Self-abuse is the path to peace"

These negative affirmations and destructive thoughts were the driving force behind much of my life. Working to subdue this rampant toxicity was a long and painful process. I had to peel back many emotional layers to find my truth and fight off these demons that controlled me and drove me down this destructive path. My daily schedule was not like any other kid growing up. As you read my book, you will see that my childhood was a daily maze of dysfunction. There were a lot of dead ends that resulted in violence and conflict. As you will see, I not only had to negotiate everyday life, I had to survive it. From the time I opened my eyes to the time I went to bed was pure pandemonium.

The purpose of this book is not to wound worship my childhood trauma, or to bring about how bad I had it as a kid. I am writing this to assist and encourage people who have had traumatic events in their lives to look at their feelings and dissect those emotional blockages. Leaving them bottled up inside one's heart will result in them festering inside you and coming out sideways later on in your life as it did for me. This was, and is a life journey for me. As I said before, the road is long and hard but it is an investment into yourself. My hope is that this account of my experiences can inspire you to adopt a more positive outlook on life, feel more grateful, and bring more love into your life. Please feel free as you venture into my heart and enjoy my journey to let your emotions flow. That is the first step of the process. Happy reading.

PART 1

Chapter 1

The Morning Purge

The footsteps trudged down the hallway becoming more pronounced as they got closer to my bedroom door. The gated limp of a large zombie-like presence stumbled past my bedroom with a sense of urgency. Moaning and gagging for air accompanied the struggle for the entity to stay upright. The only true analogy for these horrific sounds would be an exorcism. That large presence was my father Butch. Having consumed a case of cheap beer the prior day while eating very little, his gut had a consistent compulsion to expel the gallon of alcohol from the same hole that it had entered. Unfortunately for Butch, his body had a preference for the rougher means of excretion.

Anyway, my father stumbled to the bathroom at the end of the hallway and collapsed at the toilet. What came next was the most God awful sound. A shriek that rocked the very foundation of our family's morning. The morning ritual would start with some loud gagging and the periodical exclamation of expletives. This overture went on for about three minutes. Then came the purge, which was the emptying of his gut where all the beer from the previous day was rotting. Once his belly was empty, my father heaved a great sigh of relief. He would then gargle a cup of mouthwash and start his day.

My brother and I knew that after Butch completed his morning ritual, we had to make a move to get into the bathroom. There was a brief window for one of us to brush our teeth and get ready for school before our mother would have to use the toilet. My mother also drank, but her preference was gin and vodka rather than inexpensive beer. The unfortunate thing was that she suffered from Crohn's disease and her medicine specifically said "No Alcohol" on the bottle. Needless to say, she did not care. She would start drinking around noon and stop just before going to bed. The combination of hard liquor, crappy diet and Crohn's disease created a tragically unique formula in my mother's gut. The result of this intestinal concoction was something I'd rather not describe, but is necessary to understand the perverse yin and yang that was created by the upheavals of my father and the lower releases of my mother.

Over the eighteen years of my childhood, my parents created a biological system in the AM. While my father was throwing up, my mother would prepare his egg and toast for breakfast and also make his lunch for work. Once Butch finished in the bathroom, my mother would rush to the bathroom in writhing pain. She moaned and groaned while briskly striding to the bathroom, where she would immediately slam the toilet seat down and shriek in pain from the cramps. I'm not sure which bathroom visit was worse between the two. The sounds of agony lasted for about five minutes. I am sure the bowel movements would have been tough with just Crohn's disease, but the addition on drinking hard booze while on medication created a feeling that I wouldn't wish on anyone.

Now that Round Two was over, it was time to attempt a bathroom trip if I did not get in the first time. However, entering the bathroom at this point was no easy task. You must take into account the foul stench of the vomit mixed with the acidic smell of diarrhea all wrapped up in the only bathroom in the house. It goes without saying that over the years I built up a tolerance for this wretched odor.

The odd thing about these morning events that unfolded for most of my childhood is that looking back, I realize that most normal kids had an alarm clock or parents to wake them up. Even a farmer has a rooster. I had an alarm in the sound of ear-piercing, painful shrieking. Some days were worse than others. The severity of the given bathroom trips often dictated the quality of day to come. If my parents had a relatively easy time at the toilet, I considered that a good start to the day. A rough restroom visit usually meant that it was going to be a long, trying day because they would have an upset stomach until the evening.

It is one thing to start your morning off like this every day, knowing that if you just got through the AM ritual the rest of my day would be fine. Not so fast! This was just one of many obstacles that I had to negotiate daily from dawn to dusk. I truly had to earn my pillow time.

Chapter 2
The Affair

As a kindergartner, I had a relatively normal life in central Massachusetts. I lived in a plush two story home with my own room. We lived on a lane that was entirely owned by my grandfather, and the other two houses on the street had our family in them. Their houses were even nicer than ours, including pools and fountains to go along with a large field surrounded by towering maple trees. I had an older brother in 2nd grade who I had decent companionship with. My mother, Joanne, was a stay-at-home mom that maintained the house, cared for our animals and cooked meals. My father Butch provided for the family as a welder. Becoming a steel worker was a relatively fruitful occupation for a former Navy sailor who never graduated high school. His real name is actually Warren, but Butch was his preferred name after acquiring the label from his dad.

This stable, somewhat privileged family dynamic was completely uprooted one fateful afternoon, and from that day on my life was dramatically changed. I specifically remember playing with matchboxes in my room quietly when I started to hear screaming downstairs. I ran down to see what the problem was. I was acutely frightened because I had never really been around violence before, so I peeked around the corner to see the cause of the commotion. What I witnessed that day was the first take of a scene that was reenacted seemingly every day for the rest of my childhood and teenage years.

I have always referred to this fight as the "big one" because at the time it was so foreign to me that it has been seared into my brain ever since. Although there were hundreds of fights, some of which were more violent than this one, the first fight about the affair was by far the most memorable.

When I peeked around the door, I saw Butch screaming at my mother about sleeping with another man. My mother was denying it while crying and pleading her case in her most agonizing, shrieking voice. The screaming match quickly transitioned into a physical altercation with pushing and shoving. I had no idea how to process this situation, but all I knew is that I wanted it to stop. I eventually mustered up some courage and stepped out into the middle of the door where they could see me in plain sight. Unfortunately, the fighting had escalated to the point where seeing me didn't matter.

Butch started poking my mom in the chest with his finger while barraging her with insults. At the same time, my mother was trying to hug him and get him to calm down. Butch kept rejecting her advances by pushing her away, which gradually progressed into forceful shoves. At this point, my mom realized that her peaceful appeal would bear no fruit, so she started to push back in an attempt to protect herself. As the pushing and shoving continued, I had to tap into my depleted storage of courage in order to make an impact on the situation, and I decided to step in and break them up. This is an important time to note that my parents were not average sized people. This heavyweight matchup featured a 6'1 steel worker with massive arms and a military background in one corner. In the other corner was a 6'2 Italian woman who weighed over 200 pounds. As a five-year-old who weighed less than 50 pounds, I had inserted myself as a referee in a fight that I had little physical capability to influence.

My initial strategy was to squeeze in between them and pry them apart, but this was futile due to the size discrepancy. I had to quickly adopt a new strategy because I couldn't stand the fighting any longer, so I started screaming at the top of my lungs while tears rushed down my face. My parents finally went to their respective corners fuming. However, it seemed as though my helpless intervention had momentarily broken their enraged trance. At this point I was emotionally exhausted, and I ran upstairs to my room in a panic trying to make some sense of what had just happened. The memory of laying on my bed in shock after the battle is still clearly imprinted in my brain today. About three minutes had passed before I heard the loud crash of glass breaking. Apparently, I had done little more than delay the inevitable. I ran down the stairs to find that my parents had resorted to throwing vases and pans at each other from across the room. It really was like a dodgeball match, but anything qualified as an acceptable projectile. At this point, I had no idea what to do, so I just screamed at the top of my lungs: *STOP!!!* Again, I ran up the stairs and buried my head beneath my pillow and just prayed for the fighting to stop. My prayers were answered as everything calmed down shortly after I went upstairs. The next thing I heard was the front door slamming. For the third time, I slowly crept down the stairs to see if the dust had cleared.

I cautiously scanned the room where the battle had taken place, feeling safer knowing that someone had left the house. I noticed my mother balled up in the corner on the floor sobbing. I immediately went over to give her a hug in an attempt to console her. There were no words exchanged, just tears of sadness and relief that the ordeal was over. As a five-year-old, I really didn't know about affairs and all the other sexually vulgarity I heard that day. All I knew was that I had an instinctual yearning for peace. From that day on until I went into the army at 18, this would become one of my daily chores: to break up my mother and father from their battles whether small or large.

Needless to say, my mother and father separated following this clash. We had to move out of our 3000-square foot house in the country that was gifted to us by my grandparents. Ultimately my mother, brother and I moved into a tiny apartment in the city, and my father moved in with his family. These were such confusing times for me, as I really did not know which end was up. I skipped the rest of kindergarten that year and tried a new school the next year. I remember being so depressed that I couldn't engage. While my parents were separated, I moved four times during the span of kindergarten and 1st grade. In one of the towns, I lived in this run down duplex and finally went to school for 1st grade. At this point, I had decided in my heart not to make friends. This was a protective measure because I knew that I would likely be moving again in the near future. Even when kids would try to be friendly to me, I would shut down their advances and keep to myself.

In this school, I also remember getting a special voucher for school lunches which I didn't understand at first. This was really the first indicator of the impoverished conditions that were to come for my family. Eventually I discovered that my mother had no money or job to pay for food. We also started going to a special food bank to get all of our food. Most of the food in this special store had white labels that just had one word on can describing what the contents were. During this time, we made the transition to drinking powdered milk. However, my brother John refused to drink it. All he would eat was the white label peanut butter on burnt toast. I never found out why he had such a preference for having his toast burnt. For most of that year we lived on peaches, water, bread, peanut butter, and powdered milk. Our vegetable consumption came from canned corn and green beans in the evenings. My father would not come to visit us for a year and I really missed having a family.

After a year, Butch came to visit us at our beat up house. I remember him not wanting to come in, but fighting through this aversion out of the desire to see me and my brother. After talking with us, we convinced him to come speak with Joanne. I made sure to be especially cordial at first so he would visit more often on weekends. He started to visit more and more, until eventually he stayed overnight and decided to live with us again. At long last, our family had been reunited. I had sorely missed the presence of both of my parents being at home, and this was a time of great excitement for me. After moving five times before I started 2nd grade, we moved to a nicer duplex in another city closer to my father's work. I finally had some normalcy back in my life, or so I thought.

I noticed my mother and father were relatively normal in the morning but were much different when night came around. They became aggressive and combative as the sun went down, and this hostility was accompanied by them slurring their words. I could not make sense of it until I realized that my father was drinking canned beer and my mother was drinking hard liquor. The constant moving created enough instability on its own, but the alcohol put my family in a perpetual state of imbalance.

Chapter 3
Sharp Objects

In the early grade school years when I went to school, I noticed a complete metamorphosis in my mother and father from morning to evening. Even while they dealt with their hangover ailments, my parents were still amicable in the morning. In fact, they would act as though nothing had happened the night before once they had purged the toxins from their systems. Perhaps it was their inability to remember the previous night that allowed the vicious cycle to play on a loop for the rest of my childhood. It was like each of them had found their own personal Dr. Jekyll formula that would transform them into their Mr. Hyde version by night.

In the morning they were both cordial like nothing happened, but come 5 o'clock their tone and attitude would completely change. My mother started slurring her words when the evening came around. My father would reciprocate this same energy when he got home from work, usually burping and passing gas as well. After an hour or so, we would eat the dinner that my mother had prepared. Butch would always make sure to compliment her on the cooking. However, this merely served as the calm before the inevitable storm. As soon as supper was over, the festivities of the night would begin. Usually it would start with something as simple as a negative comment. It only took one small spark to trigger the forest fire. An initially novel disagreement would devolve into the same argument that I heard for the rest of my childhood, when Butch would bring up the affair. It was like a broken record, playing over and over again. I often would sit on the couch watching the TV just trying to understand why this kept happening. My brother would take the same approach that he had taken on the night of the first big fight, which was to disappear into the confines of his room. This was the strategy that he stuck with for the rest of our upbringing.

My brother's apparent apathy combined with the relentlessness of my parents compelled me to continue playing the role of referee. They would go back and forth about the affair, and Butch would mention the man's name that had the affair with my mother. DOWEY! Whenever I heard this utterance, I knew I was in for a long night. My mother would constantly deny Butch's allegations about being with another man. The typical argument would start with them slurring obscenities at each other from across the room. Their voices would get louder with every sip of their liquor. By the time that an hour had elapsed since dinner, it was a full on screaming match. It only took about six months of our family being back together for it to start falling apart again. The evenings started to wear on my spirit. The arguments were a beast that I had to face on a daily basis. I would be in the same room as them and let them yell at each other, in hopes of the tension eventually dying down. This never really came to fruition though, as things would always slowly take a turn for the worse.

The verbal conflict would become physical. As soon as I saw them stand up, I knew that my role as a mediator had shifted to being a boxing referee.

Being of similar height, any physical altercation would begin with them getting nose to nose with each other. That was my queue to head them off at the pass before anything serious could happen. At first, I would just get up and yell at them to knock it off. My youthful optimism and innocence helped me believe that this verbal interjection could prevent the festering of the deep wound that my parents were dealing with. When that tactic didn't work and they decided to start a shoving match, I had to separate them.

As I mentioned before, their sheer size made this a daunting task for most of my elementary school years. Prying these two enraged behemoths from each other's grip was like trying to rip an octopus off its prey. If I couldn't separate them with pushing, then I had to resort to punching. While they recklessly swung at one another, I would target whoever was actually making contact with their strikes. I usually would aim for the arm or back, but in some cases I went for the stomach in order to briefly put them out of commission. As the brawls escalated, I sometimes had to draw the anger towards me and to distract the two livid lunatics. Realistically, Butch could have killed her with his bare hands. He actually got kicked out of the Navy for beating up two fellow sailors in a bar. They were hurt so badly that they needed medical discharges from the service. This mix of military experience, strength, and rage made it so he could quickly take out a target. However, he wanted to make my mom suffer for her infidelity. This allowed him to torture her with conflict and fear time and time again, night after night.

When the fights resorted to head blows, I would get so incensed that I would go completely nuts on them. I got to a point, around 6th grade, where I could outmatch their craziness. When they saw me go mental, they would retreat to their corners and wait for me to calm down. I guess my temporary lunacy would help snap them out of their deranged trances. When I got them to calm down, I would give them orders on what was going to happen next. Usually, I sent Butch to my room to sleep. I slept in the same room as my mother, to serve as a deterrent for my father. It was an attempt to protect her in case Butch snapped in the middle of the night and decided to start up the fight again. If this did end up happening, I would yell at him to get out of the room, and got physical with him in order to keep him out until he finally relented.

There were an innumerable amount of fights throughout my developmental years, but a select few stood out that really epitomized the dysfunction. The one that I most vividly remember was a brawl that happened when I was in 7th grade. I was upstairs in the kitchen and my parents were downstairs in the basement. Out of the blue, my mother started desperately screaming for help.

She was yelling "He's got a knife." "He's going to kill me." I rolled my eyes as I was making a PB&J sandwich, thinking "here we go again". By this point I had become somewhat numb to these traumatic occurrences. Despite my initially indifferent reaction, I knew that I had to take on the parent role and separate the quarrelsome children. Unfortunately, this fight was not just a standard fire drill.

When I opened the door to the basement, the first thing I saw was my mother running to top of basement stairs in a complete panic, crying hysterically. Butch then appeared at the bottom of the stairs and was screaming at her "I'm going to fucking kill you!" This was not a unique phrase to his conflict vocabulary. I had heard this song and dance before, but this fight was different. As I watched this unfold with my mother at top of stairs and Butch at bottom, I noticed that he was holding a huge scuba knife. Mind you, this is no ordinary kitchen knife. This is the kind of blade you want when you are wrestling a shark. All my years of experience had prepared me for this moment. I weighed all the variables in a split second and knew I had to protect my mother. I knew yelling and pleading wouldn't do the trick this time. The only means of preventing tragedy was to disarm and disable Butch. As my mother passed by me through the door at the top of the stairs, I screamed at her to run to her bedroom and lock the door. I then focused my attention back to Butch, who was halfway up the stairwell wielding his massive blade.

I immediately slammed the door that separated the basement stairs from the upstairs kitchen. I then braced myself against the door to prevent him from getting through when he reached the top of the stairs. At this point I didn't have much of a plan, but I knew that when that door opened, violence and bloodshed would ensue. When Butch got to the top of stairs, he started violently slamming on the door with full body blows. After five or six of his slams against the door, I decided that I wouldn't be able to hold him back for much longer. I had to mentally prepare myself for what was going to break through that door. My obstruction clearly hadn't made him calm down, and was likely having an inverse effect to my usual intervention. This was a potentially murderous frenzy. I knew that I would have just one chance to punch him as hard as I could in the face. If I landed a successful strike, all I could do was hope that he didn't get up, otherwise the next person in his path would likely die.

I let him pry the door open just enough so his face and head were showing. The visual was much akin to the scene from the Shining when Jack Nicholson's face was peeking through the hole in the bathroom door. As soon as I saw a glimpse of his face, I cocked back and unleashed a devastating blow. I punched him with all my might square in his mouth. I had punched this hard in the past, but never in the mouth. Butch stumbled back and then fell down the near 20 step stairwell. I opened the door to see what was to come next. As I looked at him at the bottom of the stairs, I realized that he was still conscious but very subdued. His hands were covering his mouth, but the blood was oozing through his fingers.

Although his anger remained, the fact that he didn't immediately continue on his warpath indicated a potential shift in his mindset. He looked up and saw me at the top of the stairwell. This was a piercing stare that I'll never forget. What came next was a relatively positive revelation considering the context. Butch yelled at me at the top of his lungs, "you broke my fucking false teeth you mother fucker! Get the fucking superglue so we can fix them!". This happened as he was spitting his dentures into his hands in multiple bloody pieces. I raced to get the superglue and a towel, hoping that my quick assistance would help prevent any more violence.

While Butch went to the bathroom to inspect the damage to his face, I went to my mother's room and informed her that the fight was over. I told her that she should come out now so she can help me and Butch reassemble his false teeth. After about five minutes, Butch came out of the bathroom with a clean face and my mother came out of her bedroom to assess the damage. This was getting back to the regular routine after a physical battle. I got a paper towel and a bowl of water to clean the puzzle of teeth and gums. I sat down at the dining room table and asked Butch to bring me his dentures so that I could attempt to reassemble them. He walked over to the table and placed them gently on the paper towel. He sat down next to me at the table with a subdued demeanor, and I felt a massive sense of relief. This especially eventful fight was finished.

Butch began carefully cleaning the blood and debris off of his artificial teeth. With tensions having eased, I called my mother over to the table to assist us. I tasked her with drying off the seven separated parts of my father's mouthpiece. From here, we were able to create an assembly line. How such functionality arose from the recent peak of dysfunction that we all had just been through, I will never understand. I guess it was part of the irrationality of it all. When Butch finished washing a piece, he would pass the clean product to my mother for drying and inspection. When a piece was ready, it was passed to me for the gluing phase. I took this role because I had developed a steady hand from my art skill and extensive experience with sculpture clay.

Now that I had received the two denture pieces, I took the small tube of super glue and began to reconstruct my father's face. Butch briefly started to bicker with my mother, at which point I immediately intervened by yelling "shut the fuck up! NOT NOW" at the top of my lungs. They both quickly got quiet, and returned to tending to their assigned task. After about 20 minutes of my best attempt at cosmetic surgery, I looked at Butch and said "boy you got your ass kicked by a 13-year-old!". The three of us looked at each other and just broke out in laughter. For the remainder of the project, we were joking and having fun at the dinner table like nothing had happened. If this is not the epitome of dysfunction, I don't know what is.

Many of the fights were self-contained adventures, but there were also times when the police got involved. The aggregate of police interventions probably averaged out to about once per month. It was often our neighbors who would call the police when the conflict became obnoxious and was sustained over longer periods of time. Our frequent moving, 13 times from kindergarten to tenth grade, made it so we didn't really have established rapports with our various neighbors. The fighting that produced these calls to law enforcement often occurred when I wasn't home to mediate the situation. My mom would also call the police on occasion, but there were obstacles of the time that made this hard to pull off. Calling the police wasn't as simple as just pulling out your cellphone and making the call. You had to go to the room with the corded rotary phone and physically dial the phone number. Needless to say, the restrictiveness of the cord made it hard to make a call while involved in an intense conflict.

If the police did show up at our home, they would take Butch down to the station if he was still around the house. However, Butch was savvy enough to flee the scene if my mother managed to make it to the phone and call the police. There were times that the police showed up and I was still home, and they would look me in the eye and tell me that I was in charge of the house for the time being. Even though my brother was older than me, his disinterest and lack of involvement led him to never be around for these situations. In all the different places I lived as a child, I always accepted this role. Despite all of the arrests, my mother never had the courage to file charges against him. She certainly qualified as battered and bruised, but I think her guilt about her affair kept her from pressing charges.

chapter 4
Car Rides and Dive Bars

Car Rides

Being at home was the source of the most horrific fights. However, it was the family car rides that were the most consistently dangerous scenarios. Not only was my family packed into one confined space, but any conflict had the potential to result in tragic externalities to others on the road.

The most memorable car moments came in our beat-up Datsun B-210 that we had for almost a decade. For those of you unfamiliar with this old-timey Nissan, the Datsun B-210 was similar to a Honda Accord. Our little jalopy came complete with a patchwork Bondo paintjob, occasionally functioning headlights, a permanently cracked windshield and dented bumpers. It was really my father's car since he was the only one that knew how to drive a stick shift. Any family car ride was kind of like going on an African safari: you didn't know what beasts you would encounter. The only difference was that our threat would be internal. When the four of us got into the car together, the one constant variable was that my parents would be drunk and itching for another argument. If the car ride was going to be any longer than 20 minutes, I had to mentally stay ready for some action.

Butch's driving routine was to have an open beer can between his legs and a cigarette in his left hand while sporadically steering with his right hand. My mother sat in the passenger seat, usually holding an unmarked cup of gin or vodka. Staying true to his brand, my brother would have his headphones on to ignore the inevitable conflict. He always sat behind my mother on the right side of the car. This left me in the seat behind my father, which was a spot that came with a lot of responsibility. If things got crazy during the trip, I was in position to restrain my father. It always started with Butch verbally probing my mother about the affair. By the time the evening came around, my mother would be intoxicated enough to tolerate Butch's criticisms. We typically went places at night because my father worked during the day.

A fight would get going when Butch started to scream at my mother, which would progress into him aggressively poking her. She would start yelling back and pushing his hand away. Mind you, we are still driving during all of this. When things got to this point is when Butch's swerving would get dangerous. If he had the awareness to remember that driving was the number one priority, then he would spit on my mother because his hands were on the wheel. When he spat on her face, my mom would get extremely agitated and proceed to start hitting Butch. This is where I came in. In order to break them up, I would unbuckle my seatbelt and climb to the middle console to put myself between them. I did whatever I needed to do to keep the peace. Sometimes this could be accomplished with yelling, but other times required slapping or even punching. I tried to keep methods proportional to the degree of violence from my parents. Even the commotion of this claustrophobic conflict couldn't get my brother to take off his headphones.

This riskiness of this juggling act was further compounded by the fact that we almost always took backroads with no street lights. As I mentioned earlier, my father didn't care much to make sure the headlights were functioning, so visibility was scarce on these less traveled routes. This was actually part of Butch's strategy, as he wanted to avoid running into the cops. This was motivated by two primary reasons, which were his drunkenness and lack of headlights. He was both driving drunk and drinking while driving, so it would have been extremely troublesome if he was ever pulled over. The constant wrestling match in the front seats led to intermittent swerves into the other lane of these dark country roads. Every now and then, there would be a car coming in opposite direction that couldn't see us coming at them. It was miraculous that we never were part of a deadly accident. I'm pretty sure that God was our co-pilot every time we got into that car.

Dive Bars

The car rides that my family took were an adventure in their own right and did not need a destination to qualify as such. With that being said, one of the most frequent endpoints of our rides were the local dive bars located around our current home. These shady restaurant/bar establishments oddly provided a great outlet for both of my parents. This in no way meant it was a healthy method.

There was one dive bar that was particularly wild, although it wasn't one that we had to drive to. It was divided into two sections. The part of the Bar was the adult section where beer could be ordered and consumed. The other part of the restaurant was used for eating, bingo, and pool. On Saturdays, my parents and I would walk across the street to this dive. Of course, they were already adequately inebriated before we arrived. Despite their drunkenness, their first move was always to go directly to the bar for their gin and cheap beer. I also had a routine, which was to claim a table and prepare for the fireworks which happened almost every week.

Following her initial visit to the bar, my mother would come to the table with her drink and a soda for me. From here, she would prepare her bingo card and chips for action. The juke box was usually playing some sort of Elvis music way too loud, which set the stage for my mother's upcoming obnoxiousness.

Meanwhile, Butch would take his beer over to the billiards area where he would compete in pool for cash. The normal challengers were local bikers, who were also drunks. This informal betting for cash not only for pride, but also to have cigarette money for the week. So as Butch was playing pool, the Bingo would get going. When they started calling numbers out, my mother would get energized with excitement. Every time my mother got a number called on her card she'd scream out "Got it!". The rest of the low-life people in the bar got visibly annoyed with her because she was so loud, but stopped making any comments towards her because of her persistent indifference. This was also aided by her large size, willingness to yell back at them, and the fact that Butch was usually the Alpha male in the bar.

As a boy in my elementary years, these bar encounters was pure entertainment. This was literally the only time my parents worked as a team to put bread on the table. It was also an opportunity for them to take out their energy on people besides each other. I would just sit back and sip on my soda, waiting for the imminent fireworks. My mother had the best luck in Bingo and would win often. I have no idea how she did it. The prizes were usually a pot roast, a fully baked chicken, or cash. Winning in bingo was truly the highlight of my mother's week. It was her way of contributing to our family's food supply. When she won, she let the entire bar know with the loudest "BINGO" you can imagine. This was followed-up by a long commentary on what she won and cheers of O.M.G. while she galloped to the bingo caller for her prize.

Now as the Bingo shenanigans were going on, I would occasionally look over and see how Butch was doing in pool. My mind set at 11 years old was that if Butch and Mom had good winnings on the day, it may be a calm night at the house. Conversely, I knew the hardship that awaited if they both left as losers. In the billiards area, there would often be arguments or even brief scraps. The potential for chaos was indicated by yelling and screaming from that area. This typically stemmed from one of the pool players not wanting to pay off their bet after losing. When these fights did break out, it was often my father pinning a biker against the wall with his pool stick until they paid up. They always paid after this. The bingo caller would stop calling numbers so that everyone could watch the mayhem. It was our form of white trash entertainment that embodied the way of life where we lived. Butch was pretty skilled with the cue stick, so he was usually on the winning end of these games. Once the dispute was settled, the bingo caller resumed calling numbers as if nothing had happened. My mother was so proud of Butch when he picked fights. She was probably extra excited to not be on the receiving end of his beatings. We both watched with confidence, knowing that he would easily handle himself.

At the end of the night, my parents would collect their winnings and we would head home. I shifted into peacekeeper mode for this journey. One of the key duties of this job was to guide my parents, as their drunkenness would make them stumble around aimlessly without my guidance. Getting home in itself was an act of God. Once we got home, I prepared myself for the remainder of the night. This was based on an evaluation of how drunk they were mixed with their respective winnings for the night. If they both had a bad night in bingo and pool, my father would usually bring up my mother's affair and it was game on. At this point, I shifted back into my boxing referee role and got ready for the upcoming bout.

Chapter 5

Raining Cats

As I sit down to write this chapter, I realize that I have been procrastinating on writing this section for more than a week. I now recognize that I was afraid to stir up the dust that had been long settled in my heart. This is by far the hardest thing I have ever written in my life. After 20 years of deep personal work on myself, I have learned that much of my truly dysfunctional behavior stems from what you are about to read. Before I start, I want to warn you that you should brace yourself for potential heartbreak while reading this. With that being said, I feel that I must paint this picture in full detail in order for the story to properly resonate.

It all started in 3rd grade. By this point we had accumulated four adult cats in the house, with three of them being female. The "problem" was that these female cats kept having kittens in our home. They were so cute when they were born, truly precious animals. I vividly remember the first time that this cat conflict bubbled to the surface. I woke up to sound of one of the momma cats, who had recently had a litter, crying out in anguish. I jumped out of bed and ran to the bathroom where her kittens had been, but none of them were there. It was just the mother cat, sitting next to the toilet crying out for help. It quickly became clear to me that she was crying because her babies were missing.

I hustled outside to investigate, and I saw Butch doing something odd with his car. He had the car running, and was holding a paper bag up the tailpipe of the car so that it sealed tight around the pipe. I ran up to him in a panic and asked him if he knew where the kittens were. His reply was truly horrifying. He told me that they were in the bag, and that he was putting them to sleep. I cried out "you're killing them??" in a painful shriek. He yelled "yes!" back at me, and I demanded to know why. Butch replied, "because we can't afford them". He also explained that the gassing process would be painless for the kittens.

Because I was petrified of Butch, I watched in agony as he tortured the innocent creatures. After about five minutes, he took the bag off the exhaust and looked in the bag to see if they were dead. He then threw the bag on the ground and went into the house in a hurry. While he was in the house, I quickly checked the bag to see what had happened. The kittens were still alive, but were desperately gasping for air. They were three or four weeks old at this point, so they were fully developed kittens. A mother cat doesn't leave the litters side for a week or two until they are a little more developed. Butch understood this, and waited until the time when the mother cat would start leaving their side so he could snatch them up. As I waited outside with this bag of suffering kittens, I could hear the mother cat inside crying for her babies. This was so devastating for me, as I really loved my pets. They were my best friends and often slept with me at night. I fed them, laid with them, and they reciprocated this love back to me. Needless to say, this was absolutely killing me inside.

Butch came rushing out of the house with a rectangle laundry basket, the kind with an open air plastic screen on the side, as well as a cookie sheet. He took the paper bag with the kittens and dropped it in the basket. He then put the cookie sheet over the bag in the basket and started to give me instructions. At this point, the kittens were desperately meowing in agony for air. Butch gave me a direct order to take the basket of kittens across the street to the nearby pond. When I got there, I was to dump the seven cats out of the bag into the laundry basket, place the cookie sheet over the kittens in the basket and then submerge them in the water. I yelled "what!" in defiance, but Butch quickly retorted by saying "do it now, hurry! They are suffering!". I barked back "why don't you do it!", and he responded by saying "I am going to be late for work. Do it now!".

Since it was summer, I didn't have school or anywhere to be, so I grabbed the basket and made my way over to the pond. It was an awkward basket to carry, but I got over there as fast as I could. There was never anyone at the pond, but when I arrived at the shoreline I still wanted to act fast so I could put an end to the kittens' misery. Without hesitation, I dunked the basket into the water until it was totally submerged. I held the basket down with one hand while pushing the cookie sheet with the other in order to keep the cats below the surface of the water. After 30 seconds or so, I pulled the basket up onto the shore to see if all of them were dead. I lifted up the cookie sheet and saw that the kittens were still moving a little but clearly close to death. It was hard to bare this visual, so I immediately dunked them into the water again. This time, I kept them submerged for much longer, dreading the moment when I would bring the basket back to the surface. At the same time, I wanted to make sure they stopped breathing so that this tragedy could be brought to an end. Throughout this entire process I was crying hysterically. I knew the task would be completed following the second submersion. I finally mustered the strength to pull the basket out of the pond. I removed the cookie sheet and looked down at the lifeless kittens that I had just murdered.

At my age, I wasn't able to fully grasp what I had just done. However, I did know that I had just killed the babies of one of my closest friend's. I looked at the dead kittens with their drenched fur and realized that I needed to bury them. Unfortunately, I didn't have access to a shovel, so I decided that I would put each of them in the pond so that the whole ordeal would be over. I felt a burning sense of guilt pulse through my body as I prepared to get rid of the kittens for good. Without further thought, I grabbed the first dead cat and began the process. The even sadder thing about this murder scene was that I had named each of the kittens when they were born and helped take care of them during their early days. So as I threw each kitten in the pond, I yelled:

"Goodbye Tigger!"

"Goodbye Peanutbutter!"

"Goodbye Snoopy!"

"Goodbye Mittens!"

"Goodbye Groucho!"

etc.

As each hit the water, I watched it sink before I threw the next one. In my own way, I was honoring each one. I remember walking home after committing this terrible crime. I was carrying the basket and cookie sheet, and thinking to myself that I was for sure going to Hell.

When I got home, I left the basket and cookie sheet outside. I didn't want to bring those tools of trauma back inside the house. I went inside to my room and slammed the door behind me. Even with my door shut, I could still hear the mother cat meowing in sadness. In my mind, she was saying "where are my children?" "where are my children?". I put my pillow over my ears in an attempt to drown out the sound. For the next five days this meowing continued. It was like an emotional arrow of guilt was going through my heart with every shriek from the momma cat.

My mother knew that Butch made me do this dastardly deed, but turned her head because she knew it had to be done. In her mind we only had two options: either kill the kittens and dispose of them, or take them to a pet shelter and pay to put them up for adoption. We lived paycheck to paycheck on a low income, so something would need to be sacrificed in order to pay for the kitten adoptions. In our household, there was only one non-essential good that was part of our budget. This was alcohol, coming in the form of beer for Butch and gin for my mother. Sadly, these were seen as essential in the eyes of my parents. The $100 it would cost to take the kittens to the shelter would basically cost their entire month's alcohol allowance. This wasn't a hard decision for them to make.

So from 3rd grade until 12th grade, one of my monthly chores was to drown kittens. It was only three weeks after the first murder session that I noticed another one of our adult cats getting visibly pregnant. I was tragically able to see the writing on the wall, even at my young age. This shows the true power of trauma. Every day that I saw that cat around the house, I knew that I would have to kill the kittens after they were born. This was only made worse because of the mutual love that the cats and I had. I still slept with them almost every night. Even though my guilt persisted, the sound of their purring at night was still soothing to me.

Of course, the three momma cats took turns getting pregnant. Over the course of spring, summer and fall, I probably made the dreaded trip to the pond 8-12 times a year for eight years. The act did get easier after the second year, but I noticed a new feeling growing inside of me. As I developed into a teenager, I started to feel a tremendous amount of hatred towards my parents. My anger always boiled in my gut as I carried the laundry basket to the execution site with these beautiful kittens which I had named and raised for several weeks. My mother would constantly remind me "It's time to do the cats" and "Don't let them get too big". I replied back "I know, God dammit! I know".

It was about the second year of this murderous ritual when I noticed the presence of a huge turtle in the pond. It stood out to me because it's head would pop out of the water in the same areas of the kittens that I threw. This turned out to be a large snapping turtle. In my day to day passing, I would occasionally see the turtle on the side of the pond feeding on dead fish and bullfrogs. Eventually I was able to deduce that this massive turtle had become aware of our kitten cycle, and had realized that it was a great feeding opportunity. The turtle was eating the dead cats, which completely defeated the point of trying to give them a peaceful resting place in the pond. Despite my resistance, I would still vividly imagine their poor little skulls and bones getting crushed by the jaws of this powerful creature. I tried to avoid this outcome by sneaking to different parts of the pond in hopes of giving the kitty's a proper burial at sea. The turtle proved to be too cunning, as his huge head would pop up during almost every session.

This horrific tradition can be summarized by the following seven steps:

1) Mother cats get pregnant
2) Mother cats give birth to kittens in bathroom
3) I take care of mother cat and kittens for several weeks until mother leaves box for a while
4) I take kittens out of box when mother has left the bathroom for a while.
5) Take kittens down to pond in laundry basket.
6) Drown kittens
7) Throw each one in pond for a snapping turtle.

This was one of my childhood chores. I figured over the course of eight years, I probably drowned over 500 kittens. I wasn't proud of this deed that my parents coerced me into, so I never told anyone about it. After many years of repeating this cycle, I discovered some information that made my blood boil with anger.

During one of their arguments, I learned that the cats could have been spayed for $50 each, but my parents didn't want to incur the expense. This was enraging on many levels, but to me the worst part was that my parents valued alcohol over the sanity of their child. I was assigned the role of executioner because of their irrationality from their addictions. This lack of awareness also applied to me, as they likely didn't know the emotional damage that this had done to me. This decision they made when I was in 3rd grade almost cost me my life.

When I was 16, I started having terrible nightmares. I'll never forget the first time that I experienced this terrible dream. This vision featured a group of skeleton kittens with flesh falling off of their bone being chased by a huge snapping turtle under water. These were likely triggered by my newfound knowledge of the spaying option and the fact that we could have just gotten rid of the cats. This nightmare was recurring for about two years. It got to the point where I wanted to kill myself because of the guilt I had in my heart for killing all these kittens.

By the time I was 18, I had a full-blown death wish, which was one of the main reasons that I decided to join the Army. There was so much anger inside of me from my childhood that my heart felt like a grenade that was ready to explode. To this day, I can never look at cats the same. Especially kittens. I didn't realize until long after that I suffered from severe PTSD. Since I was a low-income kid, I had no access for help anyway. Even if I did have the chance to receive support, I would have rejected it because of my immense shame about the cat drownings. This led me to do this worst thing possible: suppress my emotions and stuff my guilt deep inside myself. I have paid dearly for this choice ever since.

Chapter 6

Suzie

The sad truth about my pets is that there was a tremendous amount of turnover. Perhaps this was symbolic of the instability of my family. I had seven dogs that were significant parts of my childhood days, although there were more that had much shorter stints. My first dog was named Suzie, and she was with me from birth until I was thirteen years old. She was a medium-size retriever with straight black hair. She was relatively young when I was born, and this allowed us to grow up together. Suzie was my sidekick wherever I went. Every place we moved, Suzie was there for me. She slept with me, ate with me, played with me. She even greeted me at the door whenever I returned home, always with a smile and excitement. She was truly my guardian angel.

When my parents were living together and not in one of their many separations, Suzie was always first in line to break up the fist fights between Butch and my mother. As soon as she heard the ruckus begin, she would gallop to the scene of the crime. Her primary function was to bark incessantly at the two drunks. As I approached the conflict, Suzie would look at me and back away from my parents while continuing to bark. In this sense, I was her backup who provided the brute force aspect of the peacekeeping missions. Suzie would persist in her auditory assault while I fulfilled my duty of becoming a human wedge between my parents. While her involvement was noble, it likely had the negative consequence of increasing the volume of the conflicts. A short fight would usually end in five or six minutes if Suzie and I were able to intervene. I employed my proportional approach of yelling first, and then escalating to physicality if it was needed. Suzie knew that if things got too heated between the two enraged lunatics, her bark was rendered ineffective. In order to assist me in the break up, she had to use the weapon of last resort: her teeth. As a given conflict carried on, Suzie would start by nipping at the lower pant leg of Butch. With Suzie handling the lower half, I focused my attention on the torso, shoulders and head. When a fight got to this point, the goal of our intervention shifted towards diverting my parent's attention away from each other. If I ended up landing a head shot, the fight would be temporarily over.

Usually after round one was complete, we would all go to separate rooms for a short break. I usually went to my room, flopped onto my brown bean bag chair, and turned on my 8-track tape. Iron man by Black Sabbath was always my favorite song to get fired up for a potential round two. As I sat in my bean bag chair listening to music, Suzie would lay at my feet getting some much needed recovery. Her heavy panting indicated her exhaustion from barking, nipping and pulling. Time and time again, we would wait in anticipation of round two. More often than not, we got what we were waiting for. The silver lining of round two was that my parents would be exhausted from their first bout. The bell that alerted us of a follow-up round typically came in the form of Butch telling my mother to "go fuck herself". This was our signal to spring to action, and Suzie and I would run out to the living room for more riot control.

A normal fight lasted only two rounds, and the occasional third round would never have much energy to it. Perhaps the intense sweating that my parents had during these fights helped them sober up while simultaneously fatiguing them. After a battle, I would pet Suzie and thank her for her service. Once I had completed this household chore for the day, I had to shift gears towards doing my homework for school. It should come as no surprise that I had a lot of trouble focusing on my school work at night following these fights. As I got older and progressed in my schooling, I learned to compartmentalize more effectively. However, I never got anything close to good grades.

As years passed and Suzie got older, I noticed that she was losing some of her punch. She was getting really frail and weak, and her hair was falling out. When my parent's fought, Suzie's bark was increasingly muffled and her bites were clearly weakened. It also didn't help that many of her teeth were gone by this point. She must have been at least 15 years old by this time. I still remember the last battle Suzie participated in with me like it was yesterday.

It took place when I was 14 years old, as my parents were having a huge physical altercation in the living room. Suzie and I performed our standard duties as peacemakers. After the dust had cleared we all went back to our timeout quarters like usual, but there was one anomaly. Suzie didn't join me in my room, which is something that I didn't think much of at the time. These periods of conflict were not a time of rational thought or considerations. During the time between the first and second round of the fight, either Butch or my mother must have let Suzie out to go to the bathroom. By this point, Suzie was so old and skinny that you could see her skeleton in the parts of her body that had no hair left from being so old. She also had problems with her bladder and other bodily functions.

Anyhow, she was let outside to pee while the subsequent round of fighting quickly fizzled out. My parents quickly retired for the night by passing out from their drunkenness, but nobody remembered to let Suzie back into the house. On any night in the spring, summer and fall, this wouldn't have been a problem, as she would have been able to sleep outside perfectly fine. Unfortunately, this was a night in the middle of the devastating Massachusetts winter. This featured temperatures well below zero and frequent snow. Suzie probably tried to scratch on the side door of the house to come inside for a period of time, but her frailty likely prevented her from being persistent in this call for help. After she ran out of energy, she tried to make the best of the situation by finding a bush to sleep under for the night. The next morning, after my father had left for work, I was getting ready to go to school like normal. It didn't dawn on me that something was wrong until my mother asked me where Suzie was. I said I didn't know, and stated "she didn't sleep with me in my room last night". I followed up by asking "did you let Suzie out this morning to pee?". She quickly replied "no". She then said "I think Butch let her out last night before he went to sleep". She told me to check outside and see if she wants to come in.

My first thought was that it was super cold outside and that I should hurry to let her in, so I went to the side door to see if she was there. No luck. I went to the front door to see if she was there waiting to be let in. Nothing. It was cold enough out that I had to pause my search in order to get a jacket and hat to go outside. I went out and immediately started calling for her in all of the ways that I could think of. As I was calling for her, I started to get cold despite all of my layers of clothing. This is when the true intensity, and potential implications, of the cold hit me. With every call for Suzie I could see my breath freeze in front of my face. I started to get desperate because I knew Suzie was in trouble. I continued my calling for about five more minutes in the arctic air before I decided to investigate the side of the house. As I scanned the landscape, something caught my eye under a shrub. It was Suzie, and it looked to me as if she was sleeping.

Panicking because my face felt like it was falling off because the ice cold conditions, I yelled "come on Suzie, come on" in as loving of a voice as I could muster. Suzie did not respond. I realized that she probably couldn't hear me because of her woefully bad hearing. As I moved closer to her I saw that her eyes were open, so I motioned to her to come into the house. This attempt was also unsuccessful, but I justified this with the fact that her vision was worsening due to having cataracts in both eyes. At this point, I got on my knees and reached under the bush to give her a gentle shake with my gloved hand. As soon as I touched her balding body, I instantly felt like I was paralyzed. Suzie was a frozen popsicle. I became hysterical and frantically tried to wake her up, shaking her harder and harder with each breath. If I was in a rational state of mind, I probably would have realized that Suzie was dead, but my emotions wouldn't allow me to accept this. I ran inside to get my mother so she could help. She got her coat on and came outside to evaluate the situation.

When my mother got to the snowy bush, she gasped and shrieked "She's dead!" "Suzie's dead". She shook Suzie a few times to no avail. At this point she ran back inside crying "I have to call Butch" "I have to call Butch"! Of course, this was the early 1980's when there were no cell phones, only the rotary phones with long cords that were usually in the kitchen. She called Butch's work but couldn't reach him because he hadn't arrived yet. My mother then called me in and told me that I still needed to go to school. I asked "What about Suzie"? She told me that Suzie was dead and that we would leave her under the bush until Butch came home. I was completely dumbfounded by this plan. I barked back at her "leave her there?". She replied "yes Michael, if we bring her in she will stink up the house". She continued by saying that "if we leave her outside, the freezing temperature will freeze her body to the core and will be easier to bury". I burst out in tears after hearing these cold hearted words. I started to scream at her "you two fucking alcoholics killed Suzie!"

"Why the fuck didn't you let her in?"

"you fucking idiots!"

"Suzie fucking froze to death!"

"I should put you two drunks outside tonight and let you freeze to death!"

My mother was crying in desperation, pleading for me to stop. I finally relented and ran to my room, grabbed my backpack and sprinted to catch the school bus. All day at school, I remember being so angry and dejected. I couldn't concentrate at all. I was a ticking time bomb all day. Fortunately, nothing at school caused me to prematurely detonate. When I got home from basketball practice that evening, Butch was home and was outside looking at Suzie who still laid frozen solid under the bush. Of course, Butch was drunk by this time of day and was not thinking straight. I walked over to Butch to find that he was poking Suzie's frozen body with a shovel. I asked him why he was doing that? He said "I just wanted to see if she was for sure dead." All I could do was look at him in astonishment because I was completely speechless.

Butch instructed me to go get another shovel from the shed. I asked him "for what?". He snapped back "we have to dig a hole to bury the dog". I then desperately said to him, "this is Suzie! Get her cremated". He said in return "That's $100". I guess that was the going rate for cremating a dog in the 1980's, or at least was the excuse that my father employed to justify our actions. I pointed out that the ground was frozen solid and that there was also a foot of hard pack snow on top of it. Butch quickly disregarded this fact, saying "so what? We have to bury her". So we went down to the shed at the bottom of the hill, which was a near pitch black adventure because of the lack of lighting. I grabbed a shovel out of the shed, and Butch grabbed a huge flashlight so that we could actually see something around us. We then looped around behind the shed, and Butch drew a rectangle in the snow with his shovel. He told me to start digging. So as I dug on one side, he was digging on the other side. At first it was more like pickaxing the frozen layer of snow and the hardened ground beneath it. As I analyzed the scene with the flashlight propped up and aimed down at the hole, I was struck with the feeling this was less of an honorable burial and more like a crime scene.

After digging for about half an hour, the hole was finally deep enough to serve as a burial site. It was approximately three feet deep, with a length and width of four and three feet respectively. This was no small feat considering the frigid subzero temperature and the rocklike earth that we had to dig up. Butch then told me to take the wheelbarrow up the hill to the side of the house to get Suzie. I was in a state of complete unfeeling shock at this stage, and didn't even question if he was going to help. I started to hyperventilate as I grabbed the wheelbarrow and began to push it up the icy hill. Guiding the cheap wheelbarrow up the hill was a challenge in its own right, as the slippery ice was extremely hard to maintain balance on. I fell a few times trying to make it up the hill, sliding back down a little with each fall. Every time I fell, I would stay down for a moment and rest my forehead on the ice with a feeling of hopelessness. As I continued to suck in the arctic air at a rapid rate, I was finally able to summit the hill, which felt more like climbing a mountain. There was Suzie laying under the bush on the side of the house.

Without the help of the flashlight, I had to rely on the moonlight for guidance. I went over to the shrub where Suzie rested for the final time in order to retrieve her. With care, I gently slid the shovel under Suzie's back and guided her out from under the bush. She was all skin and bones and frozen like a fish stick at this point, so I just picked her up with my gloved hands and placed her in the wagon. I slowly wheeled her down the slippery slope without a fall until I got to Butch and the hole. He picked up the flashlight and pointed it at the frozen dog. He then passed me the light, finished off his beer with one final chug, and stuffed the can into the snow. Butch reached in the wheelbarrow for Suzie as I pointed the light down at her. As he was picking her up, he turned his head and gagged as if he is going to throw up. I'm not sure if this was triggered by the idea that he was picking up the dead dog, or the fact that Suzie smelled really bad. Either way, it was good to see him suffer a bit for all he had put her through. I briefly shifted the light towards his face as he was gagging and noticed that he had vomited a little. He hastily placed Suzie in the hole and made sure that entire body was inside the perimeter with his shovel. He then threw the shovel down, picked up his beer and wiped the vomit of his face with the backside of his hand. After this, he turned and started walking back up the hill. As he walked away, he drunkenly instructed me to "fill in the hole and pack it down". I asked him desperately, "aren't you going to help!?" He yelled "No! I'm hungry and cold" as he trudged up the snowy hill, grumbling to himself.

I was overwhelmed as I stood in the dark and bitter cold with a shovel and flashlight looking down at my dead best friend. Slowly but surely, I started to pick up little bits of dirt and snow and carefully spread it around Suzie. After each scoop, I would gently pack it down with my foot. I got the ground even with the top of her body, and then repositioned the flashlight so I could see the body more clearly. From here, I moved onto the final step which was sprinkling dirt over her body until the body disappeared. Tears were pouring down from eyes and freezing on my cheeks and nose. When the hole was filled, I packed it down and inspected it with my flashlight. After reaching a satisfactory level of quality, I stood over Suzie's grave and bid farewell for the final time.

As much as I would have liked to stay out there all night, the fact of the matter was that I was freezing just like she had. The outside of my body was frozen, which was contrasted by the burning feeling inside of me from my boiling emotions of anger and sadness. As I journeyed to the front door, I thought to myself about what I could say to my parents when I walked past them on the way to my room. I wanted to teach them a lesson, and also let them know how mad I was at them for their negligent actions involving Suzie.

My first gesture of disdain was to slam the front door behind me to signal to them that I was pissed off and meant business. I stormed into the living room and saw them sitting in a subdued fashion with shame and guilt written all over their face's. In a low and stern tone, I said "I don't want to hear a peep out of you tonight!". I stared both of them down, waiting for a response. A part of me wanted them to say something so that I could unleash on them. They both remained silent. For that one night, I was in charge and they were speechless. I turned and went into my room and did not hear a word the rest of the night. This was the last time that Suzie was ever spoken about, until now.

Chapter 7

Moody Parker Ghost

As I attempted to write about this particular part of my childhood, I encountered my first real case of writer's block. This helped me realize just how much fear I had built around this particular phase. It took me two weeks to get into the proper mindset to uncork the bottle of fear and put pen to paper. So here goes nothing.

I was in seventh grade, and was going through arguably the most violent time in my life with my family. My mother and father were literally on the verge of killing each other about the affair that had happened years ago. It was fairly obvious that my parents were heading towards another separation. This impending separation was one that I especially dreaded because we finally had a nicer living situation compared to the multitude of duplex's that we had moved through. It was a comfortable three-bedroom house that included a cool basement complete with pool, ping pong, darts and air hockey. The neighborhood was made up of about 100 houses of similar design. The only difference in the houses were the color. This was also where all of my best friends lived.

My house was positioned directly in the middle of the neighborhood, which made it a convenient spot for all of my friends to meet. This positioning also made it a spectacular place for all to hear my parents screaming and fighting throughout the neighborhood, especially in the summer when all the windows were open and love was not in the air. For about two years, I lived in this blue house with pink shutters. During the summer days, all my pals would come over and play in the basement with me or play basketball in my driveway. It was like heaven to me since I had friends that I loved and a nice home for the first time since our initial family home. When Butch came home from work, however, my friends quickly scattered like cockroaches. I eventually learned that they were instructed by their parents to come home when my father returned, because it was viewed as an unsafe place to be.

I was 13 years old when my parents separated again, which meant the one thing that I dreaded the most: moving. There was no way that we could afford the rent for the house with my parents separated. To make matters worse, I feared that we would have to move to a different town, which meant that I would have to change schools again. I knew that staying in the house was out of the question, so I placed my hope in the idea that we could stay in within this school district so I could at least keep all my friends. In an unexpected divergence from the rest of my childhood, my wish actually came true.

Across the main road from the neighborhood I lived in was a dreary, grey three apartment triplex. This run down shack was an eye sore for those of us who passed by it while on the way to school or to the ponds behind the shack. It was also known for housing drug dealers and drug users. What I would soon discover to be the worst aspect was that the house was alleged to be haunted. The house was known as the Moody Parker house. Moody was supposedly the owner of the house years ago, and the story was that he shot and killed himself in the house. And as luck had it, my mother, brother and I were going to rent one of the apartments in this beat up house.

So as we moved a mere block away from the neighborhood that I loved dearly, I was the most humiliated I had ever been in my life. Moving from my wonderful house and neighborhood to the dump across the street. The dichotomy was an intense source of embarrassment, but I was at least happy that there would be no more fighting due to the separation.

Being the youngest, I had no say in which room I got. The room that I was assigned was supposedly the room where Moody Parker committed suicide. Now I didn't really have any familiarity with ghosts or demons. My entire understanding of the concept was framed by an experience when my parents took me to a drive-inn movie to see "The Exorcist" as a six-year-old. Needless to say, I was petrified of anything that went bump in the night.

Shortly after we moved in, I remember being woken up by footsteps going up and down the stairs to the upstairs apartment. This was strange because it was the middle of the night, and nobody lived in the upper apartment. It was vacant. What's more, the front door to the upstairs apartment was locked and chained. Of course, the stairwell was directly next to my bedroom.

I didn't think anything of it the first night, but over the next couple of weeks I noticed it happening more and more, always at night. To be honest, I adapted and got pretty used to the footstep-like phenomenon. This wasn't the case for our pets. My two dogs and three cats, who slept in bed with me, got increasingly agitated when they heard the footsteps. This was especially true for my springer spaniel, Beaumont, who would violently growl. One of my cats would often hiss as well. Their unsettledness inspired me to investigate the situation.

After about a month of living in this new living situation, I came up with an idea to gain insight into the unexplained noises. My plan was to set up a trap during the day, so that I could identify if there was any sort of external presence involved. I went to the front door of the upstairs apartment to inspect the front door. Sure enough, the door was indeed locked and chained. I peeked through the window of the door and noticed that at the top of the stairwell, where I heard the footsteps, was another door and that was also locked with a chain and padlock. I then proceeded to booby trap the chain by putting two twigs in the chain. This made it so someone trying to come in at night would have to unlock the padlock and take the chain off the door handles to open the door. I also placed a garbage can directly in front of the chained door with a big rock on the lid. This worked to ensure that I would hear the garbage can be moved if someone was trying to enter, as they would have to move the rock first. Even if I didn't hear the person moving the rock and can, they wouldn't be able to put everything back in the exact same place in front of the door. Between putting the can back in the same spot and positioning the rock on the lid, I figured there was a very low chance that this would be possible in the dark of night time.

After a couple days, I heard the footsteps in the stairwell again. At this point, my intuition was certain that it was Moody Parker. However, I had to check to see if any of my traps had been tampered with. I quickly got dressed and went outside with a flashlight to verify that the trap wasn't disturbed. Sure enough, the garbage can and rock had not been moved, and the twigs in the chain were untouched. I also noticed that the light on the stairwell leading to the upper apartment was not on and it was pitch black. The hair on my arms was standing on end as I ran back inside. I took my clothes off and crawled back into my bed, where my dogs and cats were waiting for me. I had to maneuver my way under my covers to not disturb the sleeping animals. This was ineffective though, as my disturbance coupled with the recent initiation of the footsteps woke up my pets.

As I settled down in my bed, the footsteps continued. I checked my clock and saw that it was 3:15 a.m. The footsteps always seemed to happen around 3 a.m. I've recently discovered in research that 3 a.m. is often referred to as the "witching hour", which is associated with supernatural occurrences like demons and ghosts. On this particular night, my investigative discovery combined with the irritating sound caused anger to bubble up inside of me. This emotional surge was the courage that I needed to stand up to the phenomenon, whatever it was. I must admit that I was still afraid, but I had my growling dogs and hissing cats in between me and the stair well. Once I couldn't stand the constant noise of the footsteps and the animals freaking out, I was finally compelled to take action. I yelled "Stay fucking upstairs or down"! Despite the lack of confidence in my voice, the noise subsided. The footsteps stopped and my pets lay quiet. As I am writing this, my arm hair is standing straight up, and have goosebumps from the chills that I am feeling. I need to finish this chapter faster.

After the footsteps stopped, everything was calm for about five minutes. But after the brief intermission, the footsteps started again, this time coming down the stairs. The noise got louder and louder until it stopped, presumably at the bottom of the floor where my closet was. I knew that I had pissed him off. The reality of this presence was corroborated by the fact that my dogs started growling aggressively to go along with the cats becoming incredibly agitated. Then, some sounds of movement started emanating from my closet which separated the upstairs apartment from my bedroom.

My courage disappeared at this point, and I decided to turn over in my bed and face the wall with my eyes closed. If this thing wanted to hurt me, it was going to have to go through my pets who lay in between me and the ghost. Even with my eyes closed, I could sense that it was getting closer to my bed because of the increased anger of my animals. They stood up and moved towards the corner of the bed where the closet was. It was obvious that my dogs and cats were attempting to confront the spirit. As the confrontation began, all I could do is lay balled up in my bed and pray. I had the protection of my guard dogs and cats to keep the evil presence away from me.

My dog Beaumont got extremely riled up and clearly wanted to fight and attack something. There's no way he could see anything in the dark, but he clearly was sensing the presence of something that was not supposed to be there. Finally, the etheric entity moved either directly next to or directly over my bed, as my pets started going absolutely crazy in my bed. This couldn't have lasted for more than two minutes of real time, but it felt like an eternity to me. The encounter culminated with one last lunging thrust and angry growl from Beaumont, which was followed by complete silence in the room. My pets all jumped down from the bed to investigate what had just happened and clear the area. After their inspection, they hopped back up on the bed with me. I petted them and thanked them for being such good protectors. I did my best to ease them one at a time, because they were all visibly spooked, just as I was. At long last I got them to calm down, which worked to ease my anxiety in the process, and we all fell asleep. I believe my pets conducted an exorcism that night, using the combination of their animalistic rage and my prayers for the spirit to finally find peace. This was the last night that we ever heard the footsteps in the stairwell.

Chapter 8

Heroes

A New Drug

With the multitude of hardships that were a part of my world as a child, it was imperative that I had some sort of healthy outlet for my soul. In my early years of adolescence, I noticed that many of my pals started to experiment with drugs and alcohol. They would go off into fields or behind schools to smoke pot and drink. In an effort to fit in, I would occasionally go with them in the back of schools as they sit in a circle while passing around a joint or 40-ounce bottle of beer. When the item was passed to me, I just passed it on to the next person without taking a hit or drink. These friends that I had been hanging out with slowly started distancing themselves from me because of my objections to these activities. After a while, they secretively gathered and started excluding me from their inner circle. This was hard to cope with, as my friends had been my only real sanctuary from my negative home life. I needed something or someone to fill this void.

I remember one day in 6th grade, my P.E. teacher Mr. Kelly took me in the back gym during P.E. and said to me, "You could be really good in basketball if you put your mind to it." He asked, "do you trust me"? At that time in my life, I trusted no one, not even myself! But of course I said yes. So he tied a jump rope around my waist and grabbed my right arm and tied it to my backside. He said he noticed that when I was playing basketball in P.E., I always went to my right. So in this tiny back gym, he instructed me to dribble and do layups with only my left hand. So for the remainder of the P.E. class, while all my friends were having fun playing 5-on-5 full court basketball, I dribbled up and down the auxiliary court dribbling with my left hand. I admit that it was extremely frustrating at first, as I was making a lot of mistakes. However, that one session brought me the realization that I actually was getting better each time I went up and down the court.

This was when I discovered my own personal vice: basketball. From that day on, I asked my P.E. teacher to give me a different basketball move to work on in the back gym while the rest of my class was in P.E. He must have been able to sense that I needed this outlet, as it was abnormal for kids to be allowed to separate from class.

I immediately was hooked on this game, and it became the central focus of my attention. I started practicing the various moves after school at the local playground outdoor court. Over the days, weeks and months of consistent practice, I noticed my game getting significantly stronger. I began to dominate pickup basketball games with kids of my age. While the rest of my friends continued to get drunk or high and hangout with girls, I was getting addicted to basketball. I started riding my bicycle to other towns with outdoor courts in hopes of finding better competition. After two summers had passed, my physical maturation combined with my skill improvement necessitated that I searched out competition from grown men. My peers were not really a challenge anymore.

Heroes

MELVIN

One day I went down to my junior high outdoor court to shoot and dribble like I often did. On this particular day, however, a person that I hadn't seen before came to the court that I usually had all to myself. During the middle of my workout, a long, brown and tan Lincoln Continental pulled up to the court. Out of the car stepped a light skinned black man with a large afro. He had a matching set of hoop shorts and tank top that were accompanied by dark sunglasses. He went to his trunk for a basketball and walked onto the court, saying "hi" to me as he walked past. I was surprised to be acknowledged by someone that seemed so cool, but I was awkwardly able to say "hi" back as he went to the other hoop to practice. After I worked out a little more, I sat down to rest and watch the new guy practice. He appeared to be around 30 years old, and was in really good shape from head to toe. His athleticism was shown by his fluid movements and incredible jumping ability. I found myself feeling a sense of awe, as I had never seen anyone so athletic in-person before. Despite my nerves, I quickly came to the realization that this was the type of competition that I had been looking for to improve my skill level. It took me about 20 minutes to muster the courage to approach the man and ask him to play me in one on one.

The man gladly accepted my challenge. I got the ball first, and unsuccessfully attempted to get past his stout defense. This possession resulted in me taking a tough fade away shot that missed. The man got the ball easily scored on me. My confidence was in shambles, but I still felt like I could rise to the occasion and beat this guy. This turned out to be a delusional thought, as the game ended without me scoring a single point, and him scoring ten to win. After the game, I shook his hand and introduced myself to him. He said his name was Melvin. We got to talking about basketball for a while before returning to our respective hoops to continue practicing. This was the beginning of what would become a great friendship and mentorship. Over the course of days and weeks, we started to hang out more. We would show up to the court at similar times to work out and developed a rapport with one another. It turned out that we actually lived in the same neighborhood. He lived a few houses up the street from me, which made me think that he knew what was going on at my house with my dysfunctional family. He probably was able to hear the obnoxious fighting. Despite this, we never spoke about my family over the course of our five-year friendship. I think he was just trying to get me away from all of it.

Eventually, we decided that we should go play competitive games against other people rather than just playing each other all the time. Realistically, he probably was getting sick of beating me in 1 on 1. So Melvin would pick me up at my house and we would go play ball in neighboring towns where the competition was better. Looking back, it's pretty clear that he was training me up so I could hang with stronger competition. This was our routine for the next couple years, as we went from court to court dominating the local pickup games. One day, perhaps when he thought my game had gotten strong enough, Melvin told me that he had lined up some stiffer competition for the upcoming weekend. I asked where, but he wouldn't tell me, saying it was a surprise.

So Saturday rolled around, and he picked me up at 9:30 in the morning like he said he would. As we were driving, he said "you have worked really hard and are ready for this next challenge". This was all he would say, and the uncertainty made me really nervous. Fortunately, I didn't have to sit with this anxiety for very long, as we soon arrived at our destination. This was the military base that was next to the town we lived in. As we drove up to the front gate of the post, the guard waved us through. This was strange to me, as I didn't take Melvin for having been in the military. I asked him if he was in the Army, and he explained that he wasn't, but his dad was a veteran who currently worked for the government. That explained how he was able to get into the base. So we drove through the base until we got to a huge brick building. This didn't seem like a place for basketball, but sure enough there was a sign that said "Riggs Gym" on the front. As we were getting out of the car, Melvin reiterated that I was ready for the next level of competition. He followed this up by explaining that we were going to be playing against soldiers, commonly referred to as GI's, from all over the nation. Being a skinny 14-year-old from a small town, I was rattled to say the least.

We walked in the building and approached the front desk. Melvin was able to sign me in because he was friends with the front desk person. From what I gathered, I probably was not allowed to be there, but Melvin sponsored me with his apparent credibility on the base. As we entered the gym and got a view of the basketball court, one thing quickly stood out to me. I was the only white guy there. There were two games of 5 on 5 basketball going on. Melvin told me that there was a "Pro" court and a "Rec" court. The Pro court was for the All-Army guys and college players. The Rec court was for the average players like me, although I felt below average as I watched the game on the Rec court. Thankfully, Melvin said that we would only be playing on the Rec court.

As we were waiting to play, I watched the pro court and noticed their radiating confidence. They were talking smack to each other, pushing and shoving, and sometimes they even had to be separated. I was shocked by both the level of play and the intensity. I was snapped out of my daze when Melvin told me that it was our turn to play. To this day, I will never forget what happened next. I walked slowly and sheepishly onto the court as the next game was being set up. Once the teams were set, we took our respective sides and started matching up man to man. I wasn't in any space to be assertive about my matchup, so I just let everyone else figure it out. The guy who assigned himself to cover me said to his teammates, "Hey, I got the white dude". His teammates smiled and so did Melvin. I stuck out like a sore thumb and I knew it. At long last, we checked the ball in and the game started. The first time I got the ball, the man guarding me started to trash talk me as I dribbled. "You're not going to shoot! Your scared white boy!" he sneered at me. When I ended up passing it, his statements were reaffirmed. As soon as I passed, he started telling me that I was scared. This got me a little fired up, as I felt I was being completely disrespected. So the next time I got the ball, I immediately attempted to shoot. Unfortunately, my attempt was futile as my defender, the same guy that was talking smack, swatted my shot out of bounds. He yelled "Get that weak shit out of here chump!" All the other players laughed at me.

That was it. That was the straw that broke the camel's back. The humiliation of that moment pissed me off and made me start playing like I was in a fight. And instead of me being out of control, I was able to channel this energy into a higher level of play. This mentality enabled me to hold my own against these men. Melvin knew I was ready and prepared me for this moment. From that day on, I never looked back and always played with a chip on my shoulder. So almost every Saturday, Melvin and I would go to Riggs gym and play ball against the GI's. During the week, Melvin would still take me down to the park and play one on one and shoot with me. He trained me up so I would hang with the GI's at the gym on Saturdays. Over the next few months, the guys at the gym took a liking to me and accepted me into their basketball brotherhood. Eventually, Melvin decided to move up to the Pro court at Riggs. I knew he should have been there the entire time, but stuck with me until he knew I could fend for myself down on the Rec court.

Now that Melvin and I weren't playing together on the Rec court, I was able to become my own independent entity. Having gained enough respect at the gym, I was asked to come play ball during the week by a GI. I told him that my family wasn't associated with the military and I lived off base, which is why I had to come with Melvin to gain access on Saturday's. The man informed me of a secret passage into the base. He described a spot in the woods where there was gap in the fence. After being told how to sneak on to the base, I was extended my first personal invite to the gym. The man told me to meet him at the gym Monday at 4pm so he could sign me in. So after school on Monday, I rode my bike to the location that I had been told about. Sure enough, there was a hole in the fence. I crouched as I dragged my bike through the gap and voila, I had gained access to the Fort Devens military base. It took me another 20 minutes to peddle to the gym from that point. In aggregate, the trip to the gym from my house was about 5 miles, and it was worth every peddle. I was aware that I was coming on the base illegally, but that's what made it even more exciting.

MCI and Ghost Run

 Physical training was another critical outlet for me, especially because it gave me a more private way to decompress when compared to playing competitive basketball. I wasn't much into weightlifting, as access to a weight room was inconsistent for me. So instead, I focused a lot on running. Going on runs was therapeutic because the physical exertion could be accompanied by introspection. One of my favorite routes was shown to me by Melvin. From our neighborhood, there was a four mile loop that Melvin liked to run. We ran with ankle weights, which at the time seemed like a good idea. The first time I ran the loop with Melvin, we had been jogging for about a mile when we turned into a restricted area. Soon after, we came upon a huge prison. This turned out to be MCI-Shirley, which was part of the Massachusetts Correctional Institute system. I asked him as we turned into the restricted area, "you know that the sign back there said restricted"? He said "Yup, I know, but I do it all the time and no one has stopped me. Plus, my brother is a guard in the prison". That was reason enough for me, so we just continued our run until we reached the actual prison buildings. Just past the buildings, there were fields where prisoners were working. I noticed the prisoners looking at us when we jogged by, but I purposely averted my eyes out of pure fear.

After that run, we did many others and I eventually made that part of my training routine. Sometimes I would do it alone which really pushed me to run faster, especially through MCI for obvious reasons. I ran this loop many times, and it got to the point where I needed to change things up. This lead me to start making up work outs and running loops on my own.

The first potential path that came to mind was in the woods that were behind the apartment that I lived in when I was in 7th grade. While we had since moved, it was only a couple blocks away. There was a trail that went from the back of my old haunted apartment to the pond where I drowned countless cats. The path continued into the dark woods and through some powerlines before looping down around a small sledding hill and back past the pond near where I lived. This served as a spooky trip down a literal memory lane, but I used that to my advantage by transmuting the negative energy into motivation to run faster. I would also pretend someone was chasing me in the woods, which only further enhanced my speed. I would often run this trail at night following a fight between my parents. I would perform my typical intervention and try to break up the fight before heading out to run under the moonlight. It was a rush for me to run with all of the adrenaline that had built up during the fight. In a way, this served as a natural drug that helped me escape, both mentally and physically.

NOISE HILL

When high school finally came around, I was elated about playing high school basketball. I had a lot of confidence in my game, and brought this into the tryout as a freshman. As I entered the gym, it became quickly apparent that I was in the minority from a racial perspective. Fortunately, I was prepared for this because of my experience playing at the army base. The tryout went well overall, and I could feel my hard work paying off. The coach approached me after the tryout and informed me that I had made the team. However, he offered a qualifier by saying that I needed to work on my footspeed if I wanted to play here in the future. He suggested running hill sprints to improve my speed. I immediately thought to myself "Noise Hill". This was the name of the hill behind my apartment. It was the hill that I sled down in the winter with my friends. I had never really considered it for the purpose of running, as it was about 200 yards to the top and it covered with high grass. This didn't deter me after hearing the advice of my coach, so I started progressing my way through hill workouts. Eventually I was able to do ten sets of sprints, which I would typically do after high school practice.

At first, I came in dead last on sprints in basketball practice. This was embarrassing for me because my athleticism was misaligned with my ability to play basketball, and I felt like I was losing respect. It was also frustrating because I had worked really hard on running. Unfortunately, all of my running practice had revolved around distance, which greatly improved my endurance while neglecting my speed. This ended up working out well because it gave me a new challenge to overcome, which also meant another reason to get out of the house to train. So after a month or so, I worked my way up to finishing in the middle of the pack. By the end of the season I was finishing with the front runners. This tangible improvement inspired me to keep working on my speed, and I knew what I needed to do in the upcoming offseason.

The plan was simple: run up Noise Hill daily with ankle weights and a weight vest. Ten sets every day. I would run so hard I felt like my molars were going to burst out of my mouth. That entire offseason, all I did was run these weighted hill sprints, play basketball at Riggs, run the MCI loop, and do push-ups and sit-ups in my dirt basement. Come tryouts, my sophomore year, I specifically remember doing my first "suicide" line drill on the court and beating everybody by a full length of the court. For those of you that aren't familiar with the drill, a "suicide" is a running drill that spans the full-length of a basketball court which features consecutive running to and returning from the 1/4, 1/2, 3/4, and full court. After my dominating performance, the varsity coach came up to me and said "well I guess you took my advice." This was the first of many times that we had these types of interactions, as his acknowledgment of my hard work was something that I craved because I didn't get any from my father.

BIKE TO PRACTICE

 When I was a high school junior in the 80's, we had basketball practice on Saturday's to accompany our practice schedule during the week. This meant that I had to find my own transportation to practice on the weekend. This was somewhat problematic due to the fact that basketball is a winter season sport. In Massachusetts, it snows a tremendous amount during this time of year. Because of this, it was not usually a reason for practice to be cancelled aside from extreme cases. It is important to note that this was well before the time of cell phones and mobile communication. This only worked to decrease the likelihood of a cancellation, as each player's home phone would have to be called individually well in advance to organize it.

I lived about 12 miles away from my high school, but my only option was to ride my bike to practice on Saturday's. This served as a good warmup for practice. Snow usually wasn't really an issue because the roads were well maintained with plowing and salting. This wasn't the case on one particular Saturday though, as an overnight dumping of snow left ten inches of snow on the ground. I didn't have a ride to practice because my parents didn't want to drive in the snow, and I didn't think anybody else's parents would want to go out of their way to pick me up and take me home. All I knew is that there was no way that I was missing practice. So I put on some warm clothes, jumped on my bike and off I went through the snow. About two miles in, I came to a long strip of road called the Ayer strip, and then I started running with my bike along the fence line of Fort Devens. It snowed so much that my beat up ten-speed bike could not plow through it. On the other side of the strip from Fort Devens, I saw a railroad track that ran adjacent to the road. I decided I was going to do the unthinkable. I was going to carry my bike on the railroad ties which were somewhat cleared from train activity. So for the next 4 miles or so I jogged on the railroad tracks. Luckily, I left my house two hours early to make sure that I could get to practice on time. As I got to the end of this long desolate strip, I saw a glimmer of hope in the form of paved roads. The plows must have come through while I was doing my four-mile snow jog.

So I got off the tracks and hopped onto the main road. I pedaled extra fast because I didn't want to be late for practice, and biking didn't feel very challenging after running so far in the snow. I pulled up to my high school gym with about 15 minutes to spare before the start of practice. At this point, my bike tires were completely filled with snow. Coach Malloy was the only one in the parking lot and he was waiting outside next to his Jeep Cherokee, probably to see if anyone was going to show up. As I pulled up to him on my ten-speed bike, he shook his head in amazement and said "you didn't do what I think you did?". I said "There was no other way to get to practice coach" He said "you drove from the next town over on your bike in the snow?". I replied "Yes coach!". He grinned and shook his head, muttering "wow" to himself in astonishment. We proceeded to head into the gym, and I went into the locker room to get dressed. As my teammates trickled in, some up to 30 minutes late, I thought to myself, "Wow, did I just do this?". Coach didn't mention anything to the team about me riding to practice, but I knew that the coach appreciated my dedication to the team.

So until I was a senior in high school, basketball was my passion that occupied the majority of my free time. Most of my friends got caught up in drugs and girls. Some flunked out of school. Despite my calamitous home life, I was able to escape all of those temptations by playing ball with my new friends. Biking served as a form of training when I couldn't play, and Melvin also took me jogging to get me in better shape. I was both inspired to improve and desperate to convert the toxicity from my family into a more positive force in my life.

STEWART

There were other heroes in my life that truly saved me from the perpetual state of crisis at home. They provided a critical escape mechanism for me while I was going through this trauma. One of these men was a guy named Stewart, who just so happened to be Melvin's brother. He was in his mid 30's at the time that we met, and he was still living at home with his parents and Melvin. Their dad was a retired soldier, and was married for a long time. It appeared as though there was a strong foundation of family, although I wasn't sure if Melvin and Stewart got along.

Regardless, both of them were incredible blessings in my life. I'm not sure if they felt sorry for me, knowing what I was going through, or just liked hanging out with me because I was a nice kid. As I previously mentioned, Melvin took me under his wing first for a couple of years before I had ever met Stewart. The only reason I ever got to become friends with Stewart was because Melvin and I had an unfortunate falling out.

Even though Melvin was 15 years older than me, we still had a great friendship. We did everything together. Whether it was going for long rides in his beautiful Brown Lincoln Continental looking for outdoor hoop games, going to ice cream stands for a scoop, or hitting an arcade to play some Ms. Pac Man, we hung out like we had grown up together. This all changed during the summer of my freshman year, when my "friends" started the rumor that Melvin and I were gay. I had stopped hanging out with my peers to hang out with Melvin, and had tremendous improvement in my basketball game to show for it. Maybe they were jealous that I had gotten so much better than all of them. This rumor was devastating to me, as I knew that it could have some damaging implications. Once Melvin caught wind of the rumor, our friendship was over. We never even discussed it. We both knew that we couldn't hang out anymore. It was crazy to me that all of my "friends", who had decided to go down the path of getting high and drinking, had totally stabbed me in the back.

About a month went by, and I was just starting to get over the loss of my friendship with Melvin when Stewart came into my life. The first time we met was when Stewart pulled up to my house in his green, souped-up Thunderbird. He introduced himself and asked me if I liked to fish. I excitedly responded yes, as being able to fish again was something that I had been longing for. He said that we would be leaving early in the morning the next day, and I happily agreed. This may seem like a strange way to meet someone, but we lived close in the same small neighborhood. We had crossed paths many times, usually when he would drive by when I was outside and we would give a courteous wave to each other.

Stewart said he had all the equipment and bait, which worked out great for me as I didn't have any besides one partially disabled fishing pole. So as we planned, he picked me up at 7 a.m. and went to a local spot for brook fishing. Our target was small trout. Stewart ended up having to teach me a lot, as I had only fished in the stagnant water of ponds and lakes before. These weekend fishing sessions became increasingly regular, and our friendship subsequently flourished. This was aided by the fact that Stewart also played basketball. When it came to hoops, Stewart was just as skilled as Melvin, but in his own unique way. He was probably five inches shorter than Melvin, but had a totally different skill set on the court. This included a completely unstoppable baby hook shot. We played at the same outdoor court where I had originally met Melvin, and we would usually play a lot of 1 on 1. Despite my improvement and maturation, I never could beat Stewart either.

When we were in between games or driving in his car, Stewart would subtly bring up my family and ask if all was OK there. He must have known that it wasn't because cop cars were there weekly and a lot of screaming went on nightly. I tried to downplay my family issues without overtly lying, and Stewart seemed understanding. His open concern for my home life was a major difference from my friendship with Melvin, who would never bring up anything like that. It's possible that Melvin suggested that Stewart should hang out with me after our falling out, since he recognized that I was in desperate need of companionship and guidance. Luckily for me, this friendship sustained for the rest of my high school tenure, and was more naturally ended when I decided to join the Army at age 18.

GARBAGE MAN

When I was in 7th grade, I often went to practice basketball at my local elementary school court. The outdoor court was right by the road and had easy visibility. On one summer day, a tall, slender man with fair skin approached me while I was playing. He must have been in his 30's. Although I didn't know him, I recognized this man as one of the local garbage men. Being in a small town, most people were recognizable just from everyday comings and goings. Anyway, I had seen this guy many times, as he rode on the back of the garbage truck for the Saturday rounds. He walked up and introduced himself to me. In a very professional manner, he said "Hi my name is Tim. And you are Mike, correct?". I said "yea that's me. How did you know?". He explained that he had been following me in my basketball career, as he liked to come watch the local middle school team that I play for. He also somehow knew that I worked at a local farm, doing random jobs like chopping wood, landscaping and cleaning out pig and cow pens in order to make some extra money. Tim said that he had a job opportunity for me that might be more appealing than that intense farm work.

The gig was helping on the back of the garbage truck. Tim told me that these positions weren't usually offered to minors, but this was a special exception because Tim saw my work ethic on the basketball court. He had also already asked the owner of the farm if it was okay that I took on another job, and the owner accepted this arrangement. He then asked me if I was interested? I accepted excitedly, which caught Tim by surprise. He chuckled "you don't even know what it pays yet!", to which I responded "hey man, money is money". Tim laughed and said they could pay me $10 an hour under the table. This was good money at the time, especially considering my age. The deal was that I would work Friday's and Saturday's in the summer, and only Saturday's during the school year. I eagerly accepted the offer for the second time. Tim smiled, likely amused by my strange enthusiasm. He gave me the address to meet him, and told me that my first shift was the upcoming

Saturday at 7 a.m. After this, we shook hands and he went on his way.

I was so pumped for this job. It would be the first job that had some sort of comradery and was more official in nature. After accepting this employment opportunity, I basically had three part-time jobs: my farm job, the new garbage truck job, and local grass cutting gigs for which I had a handful of customers. I would take any job that I could get, as this was the only way I could buy school clothes. However, my biggest motivation was to buy nice basketball shoes. This money also came in handy when my mom was short on money and couldn't pay the bills. I would "lend" her money to make sure she could make her payments. Sometimes she would pay me back, and sometimes she wouldn't. It depended on how tight money was at the time, as well as her level of sobriety.

So that next Saturday, I rode my bike to the address that Tim gave me and parked my bike next to the garbage truck in his yard. This was no ordinary garbage truck, as there was a huge mural of Captain Crunch holding a garbage can full of garbage on both sides of the hull. This truck was famous in our little town. A lot of folks would come out and wave at us or wave from their windows as we drove by on our collection route. Needless to say, my friends eventually saw me on the back of the garbage truck, and the news quickly travelled through the group. I knew a lot of my friends looked down on this job, but they also knew I came from a low income family. Fortunately, none of them really made fun of me because they knew my situation. I'll admit that I was a little embarrassed to be the garbage man, but it turned out to be such a great opportunity.

When riding on the back of the truck with Tim, we would chat about a variety of things between stops. The usual topics were Boston sports and local gossip. Everybody knew everybody's business in town. We would also talk about relationships, whether it was about women and girls or my home life. This garbage truck job ended up doubling as weekly therapy for me. I looked forward to working on the truck with Tim because I could just dump all my feelings. Tim didn't judge me, he just listened and digested all of the information. When he had a constructive response, he would share his advice with me. It was a very cleansing job for me, as my emotional garbage was being processed while I picked up the town's garbage.

The other reason that I loved this job so much was that Tim and his dad Dick followed my high school basketball career. Tim came to a lot of my games in junior high and high school. Often I would be in the local newspaper in the sports section, and sometimes the front page for when I was on varsity. Tim would clip out articles and photos of me when I was lucky enough to get some press. I averaged about 20 points and 10 rebounds a game my junior and senior year. Anyhow, Tim would tape the news clippings in the garbage truck, on the back window of the cab. I really looked forward to Saturday's after games, as Tim would commend me for my performance. Tim was a hooper as well, and had good knowledge of the game which made for great conversation. Tim even took me to some Celtics games, which was a dream come true. Tim filled a huge void in my life where my parents were unengaged with my basketball career, as they were too caught up with drinking and fighting. It was cool because Tim was truly proud of me, and impressed that I could excel in basketball considering the turmoil I was faced with at home.

These five heroes were instrumental in me surviving my childhood. I believe these men were presented to me in a divine way, so that I could navigate my adolescent years without going down the path of substance abuse or violence. Of course, I had to make the choice to follow these men, but my heart always told me to trust that this path was laid out before me. These five men filled an empty, dark void in my heart with healthy, clean love. Their friendship is cherished to this day and I will always be grateful. They say it takes a village to raise a child. These men laid a path out for me so I could not only survive my childhood, but succeed in it. They simply gave me hope when it otherwise was completely absent.

PART 2

Adulthood

Transcending Trauma

At 18 years of age, I opted out of going to play basketball in college in order to join the Army. I felt that I needed to get as far away from my family as possible. I chose to go serve in Europe, which was perfect because it put the Atlantic Ocean between me and my family. The Army was where I tapped into my anger and used it to serve Uncle Sam. Ironically, being in the military was the safest place for me at the time. It provided an appropriate playground for my demons that too often wanted to come out and play.

By the end of my Army tour, I established that I had a ball of hate inside of my heart which desperately needed exorcism. All of my negative feelings were bottled up inside of me, and my healthiest option for releasing them was still extreme exercise. Running, lifting weights, or playing basketball all served as outlets for me to put my energy into. Unfortunately, it eventually got to the point that even after exercise, my anger would creep back into me faster and faster. I was reaching a breaking point when I went to see a priest about it, as I was beyond desperate. He listened to my story and advised me to go see a friend of his that was a counselor. I was reluctant at first, but after a few visits, I started to open up a little bit. In one of our sessions, the counselor told me to be on the lookout for signs in my life, and to be open to whatever they might bring. As I worked to open my awareness, I had two very interesting events happen to me. The first event was what I call the cat bridge.

One of the main causes of my anger and self-loathing was the constant nightmares about the cat drownings from my youth, which wreaked havoc on my sleep and mental health. Getting closure on my nightmares of the skeleton kittens in the water required some divine intervention. However, I first had to take personal action to initiate the healing process. I was 25 when I started to see the counselor about my anger issues that I was dealing with. This lasted for about a year. The cat dreams came up in these therapeutic conversations. I had been having them for years and they were really taking a toll on me. As I told my counselor the story behind the nightmares, I watched her face transform from professionally composed into genuinely horrified. She was completely dumfounded and hung her head with tears flowing down her face as she sat in her chair. In a brief moment of role reversal, I had to ask my counselor if she was okay. She said that she just needed a minute. After crying for a little bit, she spontaneously popped up out of her chair to come give me a huge hug.

After the comforting hug, she returned to her counseling chair and sat back down. This was followed by another minute of complete silence, although it felt much longer because of the emotional intensity of the moment. Eventually she gathered herself, blew her nose and then took a deep breath. The words that came out of her lips have stuck with me to this day. She said in a very loving voice, "It wasn't your fault, it wasn't your fault! You are forgiven".

I knew she was a religious person because of the cross she wore, as well as making inferences from some of the stories she told me. When she verbally exonerated me of my crimes, it triggered an overwhelming emotional response for me. I started crying my eyes out. At the end of our session, I thanked her, gave her a big hug and left. As I was leaving, she told me to look for signs of healing around me. I said that I would, but in reality I didn't know what that meant. This is where the divine intervention takes place.

Cat Bridge

About two weeks later, I was at my home in Seattle. My wife and I were recently married, and had very little resources. We rented this little 800 square ft. starter home from my mother-in-law. There was a short white picket fence around the perimeter of yard. Occasionally, I would see this stray cat walking around in our back yard. I didn't think much of this, but the cat did become easily recognizable to me. There was one day that featured an odd sighting of this cat. Instead of roaming the backyard, the cat was actually on our roof. It must have jumped from a tree limb near the house. I wondered what the cat was doing on the roof and how it had gotten there. My curiosity compelled me to follow it around to the other side of the roof. The cat looked over the edge of the roof and snuck into a little vent on side of the house that lead into the attic. When I realized the implications of this, I felt my trauma squeezing my soul. I knew that the cat's actions could only mean one thing: kittens. Sure enough, in the days that followed, I started hearing little meows. This only worked to make my nightmares more prominent.

There was no way to get up in the attic crawl space that I was aware of. This posed a problem for the cats because the only way out of their new home was to jump back onto the tree limb. When the kittens got old enough to walk, there was no way for the momma cat to make the leap from the roof to the tree with a kitten in her mouth. There was time before this problem would be realized by the cats, so in the interim I tried to support her. I did this by feeding the mother cat milk and food for several weeks, until the kittens were big enough for the mother to move out. When the kittens got to this point of maturation, I knew the mother cat would start bringing them on the roof. About four weeks later, this prediction also came true. I came home one day, and the mother cat had a beautiful little kitten hanging from her mouth, desperately trying to find a way down from the roof. She walked over to the other side of the roof to the tree that she used to get up and down from the roof. She knew she could not make the jump to the limb with a month old kitten hanging from her mouth. She kept pacing back and forth with periodic muffled meows.

While I watched the momma cat hopelessly search for a way off the roof, it dawned on me that that this could be the sign that my counselor had talked about. If I could save the kittens from the attic, it would somehow make up for the kittens that I destroyed. Of course this wouldn't be true from a numerical perspective, as the 5-7 kittens in the attic paled in comparison to the hundreds that I had been tasked with killing. But in principle, the idea of saving cats instead of killing them seemed like a great opportunity for redemption. Perhaps this atonement would work to alleviate my guilt and help close that chapter in my mind for good.

So I thought to myself, how can I save these cats? Climbing up onto the roof with a ladder wouldn't do, as the cats wouldn't be able to use the ladder and I wouldn't be able to bring them down all the time. I was then struck with the idea of creating a bridge. I scoped out the house and surrounding area in search of potentially connectable points. This lead me to the look at the vent hole on the side of the house, which was near the roof. On that side of the house, the fence was a lot higher than the other fence in our yard. This was likely to prevent visibility of our neighbor's house which was very tight to ours. However, this worked great for my purpose.

The distance from the house to the fence appeared to be roughly 8-10 feet. All I had to do was prop a thin board at the base of the vent that reached to the horizontal support beam on the fence. I remembered that I had a bunch of thin, long boards in our little shed in the backyard. I quickly ran back and grabbed a couple pieces of wood of varying lengths. I ran over and started sizing them to the gap from house to fence. The first few were either too long to balance or too short to reach. Eventually, I found one that was a perfect fit for the gap. The mother cat looked at me curiously as I propped the thin board between the house and fence.

Excited and proud of my handiwork, I started to gently beckon for the cat to come try out the bridge. She was clearly too nervous with me standing there, which made sense considering she was a stray cat. This prompted me to go inside and watch from the kitchen window where she couldn't see me. As I was watching from the inside kitchen window, the mother cat started taking one kitten at a time across the make shift bridge. When she got to the end of board at the meeting point with the fence, she would jump to the ground with kitten still in her mouth. This was about a four-foot jump, which was a great deal safer than their previous option.

After getting each kitten down from the roof, the momma cat relocated her offspring under my neighbor's shed. She made five trips between the roof and the shed, which meant that there were five little ones in the litter. I left the board up that night in case she needed to retrieve anything else from their makeshift home. The next morning, I went out and took the bridge down since it had fully served its purpose. I continued to leave milk out in the yard, and it would be depleted every day when I got home, so I figured she was drinking it. I felt a comforting warmth inside of me for the next few days. This was the first sign of me forgiving myself for my horrible deeds as a child. I still had unfinished business in regards to my horrible actions with kittens, but knew this was the beginning of the end. The added bonus was that my nightmares finally stopped.

Bearded Face

A few years went by and I had one of the most profound experiences I have ever had. Throughout my entire childhood, there was one question that I was constantly considering: Is God for real? After many of the tragic events that happened in my dysfunctional family, I would go outside and look up in the sky and ask "Are you (God) for real?". I then thought to myself, "if you were for real, you wouldn't put an innocent child through the shit I am going through on a daily basis". I am ashamed to admit this, but after the various fights or cat killings I would be so distraught that I would look up to the clouds and say "fuck you" to God. This was followed by phrases like "if you're up there, then shoot yourself", and things of that nature. This behavior started around 5th grade, and continued until I joined the army at 18. I grew up nominally Catholic, but just couldn't buy in to "God's existence. My trauma tested my faith, and I needed proof that there was a higher power.

My agnosticism persisted as the years went by. I got out of the army after eight years of service. I got married and had my first son soon after. I was in my mid 20's and lived in a small house in Seattle. The cat bridge experience had been a mildly revelatory spiritual moment, but it wasn't the proof that I required to answer my question about God. Eventually, I was presented with an experience that had the potential to answer my question. I will never forget the profound and divine nature of this experience.

I was lying in bed getting ready to get up and start the day. I was tasked with waiting for my two-year-old son to wake up, as my wife was already at work. The sun hadn't risen yet, so it was still hidden behind the mountains. And so I laid there in my bed, facing up in the dark. I found myself looking up at the square coiling light in the middle of the ceiling. This was before the time of cellphones where you could mindlessly occupy yourself. The stare became increasingly meditative as time passed. I could just barely make out the silhouette of the light, but all the shades were closed in my room and it was still early dawn.

It was oddly peaceful, but my serenity was suddenly interrupted. From the middle of the ceiling light, bright beams blinded me as they pierced directly towards my face. This was not coming from the light bulbs in the lamp, these were intense arcs of light that could be compared to trying to look at a solar eclipse with the naked eye. My body went limp and I was completely paralyzed from head to toe as I struggled to look up at this bright flash. I tried to put my hands up to shield my eyes, but my arms were frozen by my side and my head and neck were locked in looking straight up at the light. My eyelids could not close, so I was being forced to look into the middle of a light source that was not from a known source of this world.

This sensation caused me to lose sense of time, but realistically it probably lasted for about 30 seconds before the light vanished back into the lamp. My body was finally unlocked, so I raised my head to look around. My door was still shut tight, indicating that I was still alone in the room. I laid my head back on my pillow in shock, trying to understand what had just happened. This brief brainstorming session was cut off when the light beams reappeared even brighter than the first time.

Again, my body went limp and lifeless as I was overtaken with paralysis. This time, I immediately surrendered to this overpowering light. My eyes were franticly trying to readjust in attempt to make any sense of what was going on. After about 10 seconds, I noticed two eyes appear in the center of the light source.

The picture became clearer and clearer, and soon enough I was staring directly at a bearded face with long hair that had taken full form around the initial eyes.

So I am lying stiff as a board on my bed, completely fixated on this extremely bright light that had taken the recognizable shape of a face. At this point I had no choice but to take it in, because whatever it was had me pinned down and clearly wanted to get me a message of some sort. I was then able to look directly into the eyes of this bearded silhouette. For the next 30 seconds or so, I had a silent stare down with the eyes in the light. Although the mouth of the face never opened, it broke the silence through an etheric message transmission. This was communicated by the eyes of this bearded man, which said "believe in me, for I am real". I didn't receive the message in words, but in more of a telepathic way. That was probably the longest minute of my life.

When the message was conveyed to me, the bearded face faded away and then the eyes absorbed back into the light. After the full face was gone, the bright beams of light slowly receded back up into the ceiling lamp and the room dimmed out into darkness again. As soon as the room returned to darkness, I was able to move again. I immediately broke down and started to cry profusely. There were far too many emotions to be contained within me, so I had to let them flow for some time. For the rest of the day I was in shock, and was operating in some sort of altered state. Tears of joy and sadness periodically poured from my eyes for the next week. It took me some time to accept what had happened to me. My wish for proof of God had finally come true.

In my attempt to grasp what had happened to me, I decided that I needed to talk to someone about this. I called my priest at the Catholic church that I was married at, and scheduled to meet him the next day. As I headed to this meeting, I was nervous about what my experience might mean for my life. However, as soon as I sat down in his office I felt comfortable sharing the entire experience. It was hard to find words to describe the event, and this difficulty was exacerbated by the emotions that kept swelling up as I told the story. It took over 20 minutes for me to get it all out. After carefully listening the whole time, the priest took a quick moment to consider everything that had just been laid on him. He then proceeded to open his Bible and read something to himself. After he finished reading the apparently applicable passage, he briefly looked up at me and then looked down again and closed his Bible. He pondered some more before he finally broke the silence by softly saying "Mike, there is a reason why God has chosen you to have an experience with him face to face". I responded back "Why was I chosen"? The priest said "Well now, that will be a mystery for you to figure out. You will know the answer but only when the time is right." The priest went on to say that he has been serving the Catholic church for many years, and that he had never had an experience like the one I had. He said "I was chosen for a reason".

Warrior

At this stage of my life, I was presented an opportunity to go to a men's retreat weekend called the New Warrior Training Adventure. I had an expectation of what it was going to be like in my mind, and boy was I wrong. This three-day weekend was just what the doctor ordered. The retreat took me on a descent into my past and guided me to the most painful part of my childhood. At that point in the weekend, I analyzed these feelings that I was experiencing, and then acted on them in an intense manner to peacefully put them to rest in my heart. I realized that this initial weekend was a rite of passage into being a healthy man. The three-day course was by far the most demanding weekend I have ever been through. Upon completion and cleansing, however, I recognized that I still had a lot of work to do to look at all my other emotional wounds that had been festering inside me for years. I also learned of the demons that lived inside me which still needed to be faced.

The Warrior Weekend was a safe place for me to look into my past and revisit the darkest parts of my childhood. When you arrive at that point, the only way to expel a demon is to rip the emotional bandage from your heart and allow the healing process to begin. The suppression of these traumas is what causes them to metastasize, rather than allowing them to flow through you and run their natural course. In the weekend, processes are done to facilitate the removal of these bandages and to provoke your demons to come out and play. I won't share the specifics of the methods, as they are sacred to the program, and I don't want to interfere with anyone's future personal experience with such a program.

The chance to release a demon is a critical juncture, where you must rise to the occasion and battle with the demon until you defeat it. If you are unsuccessful, this only means that you will eventually have to confront it again. There is no avoiding them if your goal is inner peace. Each time you address a deep emotional wound, it gets easier to face it and gets less painful until the last confrontation. The last fight is when you finally kill the demon and put it to rest.

I vividly remember my initial confrontation with my biggest demon. My murder of innocent kittens as a child had created a deep impression on my heart. At that point, I was willing to die to get this festering ball of hate out of my system. Ultimately, I had to kill the emotional demon that represented the part of my parents that pressured me to do this devilish deed. It was a true emotional exorcism to say the least. As the process was ending, I emotionally put the nails in the coffin, hopefully never having to face it again. Down the road in my follow-up support group, I sometimes revisited the cats wound and ultimately came to peace with it.

When you are dealing with trauma and hardship, there is a temptation to claim victim status. This is something that I've struggled with, as feeling bad for myself served as a coping mechanism. However, I've found that the proper mindset is to view your trials as gifts rather than curses. Reframing these experiences as learning opportunities is what provides the positive energy required to battle these negative experiences. It is a fruitless endeavor to combat such demons with the force of hate and anger, as this is exactly what gives them strength. There can be no growth without hardship. This mindset shift is what provided me with the strength to relive my trauma's and come to peace with them.

As I wrote earlier, the reason that I went to this intense men's retreat is because I truly hated myself. I was gifted these dysfunctional wounds in my heart from my parents and had to heal them or face dire consequences. My father gifted me the inability to forgive, along with the inclination to express my feelings with anger and always seek revenge. The forgiveness aspect, or lack thereof, was modeled to me on almost every day of my childhood. My father refused to forgive my mother for her affair, and they were unable to find a way to settle the matter. So every time he got drunk or grumpy, he would bring it up, which would inevitably start the chain reaction that ended in an altercation. In my support group following the Warrior Weekend, I was able to work on my inability to forgive others. At its root, this problem was caused by my internal projection of the fact that I couldn't forgive myself. This revelation took months of hard work to uncover, but it enabled me to start to forgive myself for all of the negative things that I did to survive my childhood.

After conquering the forgiveness piece, I switched my focus to the revenge factor which was the next beast I had to face. This was where all the hatred and anger that Butch instilled in me came into play. Before my initial weekend in Warrior, I would immediately enter fight mode any time somebody crossed me. I was determined to leash this internal beast that had brought so much toxicity into my material life. Forgiveness and revenge are heavily related, as my newfound understanding of forgiveness helped me to quell the relentless rage that was fueled by revenge.

I'm not claiming perfection in this department, but many needless confrontations have since been avoided because of this internal work. This shows the importance of being open to cleansing your internal world, as the positive externalities in your life will be greater than you might imagine.

Another big monster that resided in Butch that he passed onto me was the transmutation of physical pain into anger. Whether it was from a fight or throwing up, the bodily pain was compounded by the emotional pain from the idea that a higher power getting back at him for all the horrible crimes he had committed. This constant example from my upbringing led me to inherit these same behaviors. I went into the army and physically destroyed myself. I ravaged my body with no regard for recovery in training, and also got into a tank accident where I severely damaged my back. I even got frostbite in the toes due to my negligence and lack of self-care. For years, I associated the horrific pain of my pre-surgery back and the frostbite thawing stages as revenge to myself. It was during this time that I had thoughts of taking my own life. This revenge piece was probably the hardest work I had to do. Overcoming this rage and despair that I felt when I was in pain prevented me from wanting to act out and destroy someone for the pettiest thing.

Next on the list was trust, which obviously wasn't cultivated in my family environment. What I've learned about trust, similar to forgiveness, is that you can't trust others until you truly trust yourself. This was easier said than done. Learning to trust myself after years of seeing my father not trusting my mother after the affair was a daunting task. This was some of the hardest work I had to do in my Warrior training. Hours of trust facilitation processes that ended in turmoil. It took over a year of hard work before I could look in the mirror and say "I trust you" to myself and believe it.

Of course my mother gifted me some huge emotional scars as well. The deepest wound came from the memory of her incessant reminders to complete my chore of murdering our kittens. Butch taught me how to initiate the killings, but it was my mother who continued the cycle and pestered me to kill them whenever the time came. Every one of her reminders felt like a knife was being driven into my heart. This was the big work I did on my initial Warrior Weekend, and it spilled over into both my individual work and group work after Warrior.

Self-abuse was another habit that I learned from my mother. The constant drinking of gin on top of her medication was confusing to me at first, but I soon realized that she had to numb herself of the guilt and shame of her adultery. She also needed a way to endure the unending abuse from my father. My takeaway from this was to abuse myself as a coping mechanism for my internal guilt. As I mentioned in Part 1, I preferred the physical abuse of extreme exercise instead of drugs or alcohol. The physical pain provided a rush that functioned as my medicine for the dysfunctionality of my life. When I felt myself suffering, I was able to forget about the other negative emotions in my heart. In Warrior, I had to do some very dark work on why I was worthy of taking care of myself. The healing process was initiated when I was able to disassociate myself from my abusive relationship with physical pain. Essentially, I didn't love myself, which created a lack of incentive to take care of myself. After making this internal discovery and working diligently to remedy it, I had another moment where I looked in the mirror and was finally able to authentically say that I loved myself.

I confronted my biggest demon on that initial Warrior Weekend, fought it and killed it. In my 15 years of deep, personal work following this weekend, I realized that I had many monsters living in the closets and under the beds of my mind. Fortunately, the Warrior Weekend had a follow-up support group where I could continue on with my internal healing process. I went to a three-hour meeting once a week for a year, and then biweekly for another year before dialing back to about once a month for the next two years. These sessions ranged from the basic sharing of stories to intense psychotherapy and role playing where I could bring my demons to the ring for a battle. Often times, a demon was compared to an onion. Each had many layers, and every layer was like a round in boxing where I had to confront, fight and overcome in order to go deeper into the onion. It was only after I battled through those layers that I was able to get to the core of the wound and look the demon directly in the eyes and put it to rest once and for all. Sometimes one demon could take several months of meetings to get to the core. Considering that each follow-up meeting was about three hours, it was a quite demanding process that took many sessions.

During these stages of my Warrior work, I had another sign which helped me to keep the faith during my deep dark work that there was hope and a higher power. After having the jarring experience with the bearded face, I began seeing more signs that were pushing me towards getting in touch with my heart and spirituality. This compelled me to start doing some personal work. The result of this work was my realization that my heart was closed emotionally. I did not feel due to this hardened heart, which most likely stemmed from my traumatic childhood.

Following some introspection, I decided that I wanted to reach out for further help. This started with the powerful initiation at the initial weekend, which was the most intense weekend of my life. It was incredibly impactful because it taught me how to open up my heart to others, and also how to feel my feelings and properly express them. This permanently opened my mind up to the spiritual possibilities of life. After what I went through as a child, I was almost completely convinced that there was no God or heaven. I needed to see proof in order to believe that something was up there besides clouds.

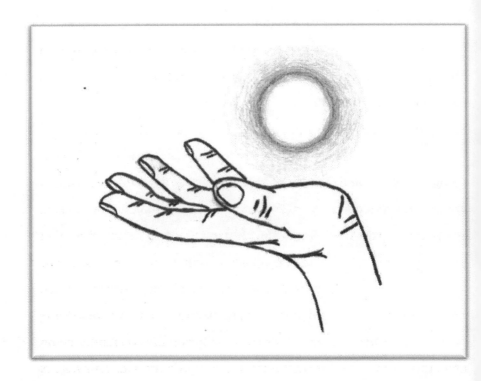

Lake Hand

About 2 years after my encounter with the bearded man, I had completed an extensive amount of deep soul work on myself and was apparently prepared for my next sign. Although I was unknowing at the time, I was finally ready to face my next spiritual experience. Interestingly enough, it took place when I was on vacation. My family and I were attending a group camping week called "Family Camp", which was hosted on Lake Wenatchee in Washington. One of the days had many of us go to a nearby lake for a day of fishing. It's called Fish Lake, and is near Wenatchee, Washington. I went with my young son, and we were fishing with some of the other kids from the camp. Fish Lake is known for its abundance of perch and trout, so it is a great spot for children to make some good catches. There is one part of this lake that is called "The Cove". This is a place where you can camp, rent row boats, canoes, and even pontoon boats. This all takes place at the quaint bait shack on the grounds, which also sells fishing gear, worms, snacks and drinks. Additionally, they allow people to fish off of their dock, which is of moderate size in the shape of a large "T". The dock juts out about thirty yards on the lake that is nestled in the mountains. The dock itself has all the row boats docked and ready for rental. The lake has a strong wildlife presence overall, including many eagles and osprey fishing from above. While fishing from the dock waiting for a nibble, you are constantly being entertained by these aerial hunters dive bombing fish. This lake is magical to say the least.

There was a man that ran the operations at "The Cove" and he truly was a fish whisperer. His name is not important, but he is a legend at this lake in my eyes. The spirit of the lake, if you will. He did everything from fixing boats, giving fishing tips, running the bait shack and much more. He must have been in his 60's at the time, and was completely bald. These weren't the traits that stuck out though. Above all, the one feature that stood out the most was his left hand. This hand was totally mangled, which happened during a snow blower accident years ago in which he lost several of his fingers. To this day, he uses that hand like it still has all of the digits. He is the soul of the Fish Lake. For over 15 years I vacationed at Lake Wenatchee with my family, and one of the things I looked forward to the most was my fishing day at Fish Lake each year. The lake was majestic in its own right, but I soon discovered that it may have been blessed with something more powerful, perhaps "holy water".

So as I was saying, I took my son and a few friends over to Fish Lake to fish off the dock for the morning. We got our worms from the bait shop and went out to the dock to claim our fishing spots. As usual, we caught a few perch, some trout, and a lot of weeds. The predatory birds were as active as ever, swooping down and grabbing fish as us amateur fishing folk struggled with the unhooking process from the dock. My son and I were located on the upper portion of the T-shaped dock, which was the furthest from the shore and on the deepest water around the dock. This was the best part of the dock for fishing, so it was a popular spot. I usually led my group to the north side of the dock as it provided somewhat fruitful yields.

Anyhow, we were wrapping up our morning on the dock, and I wanted to get a photo of my fishing crew. This consisted of my four-year-old son and two other teenage friends. I had them stand next to the edge of the dock near the water so I could snap a shot with my film loaded camera. As I took the photo, my son suddenly fell backwards under the railing and into the murky water. Where he fell in was approximately 20 feet deep. Without delay, I dropped my camera and ran to the spot where he fell in and dove over the railing into the water. At his young age, my son had very limited swimming skills. This was only compounded by the fact that he had all of his clothes and sneakers on, which meant that he was likely going to sink instead of floating. The rest of this story was a blur.

I allowed my dive to guide me about 10 feet below the surface of the murky water. After achieving sufficient submersion, I turned my attention up towards the surface of the water. As I looked up, I saw the silhouette of my son in the algae saturated water. He was completely submerged and probably 2-3 feet below the surface of the water. He was trying his best to swim, but his clothes and shoes were weighing him down. As I swam up towards him, I also began to struggle with my swimming because of the added weight of my heavy clothing. At this point, I realized that I had one shot to grab him and push him to the edge of the dock. This would require accuracy, which was tough to gauge because of the obscuring murkiness of the water. This is when I noticed, during my struggle to swim upward, that the sun light got incredibly bright around the outline of my son's body. While this worked to clarify the path to get to my son, my physical limitations were becoming increasingly problematic. It was hard enough for me to swim back to the surface by myself, so it was going to require an immense effort for me to push up the additional dead weight of my son as well. After a few seconds had passed I finally reached him and put my hand on his waist. With all my might, I tried to thrust him up to the dock. He barely budged. It quickly became apparent that I was too weighed down and my son was too burdensome. I had nothing to push off from, and had lost my upward momentum. I then realized that we both were starting to sink. I looked up one last time and noticed the light around my son's body was glowing unnaturally brighter. What happened next I can't really explain.

I can only describe it like this. A force of some sort appeared below my flailing feet and thrust me and my son to the surface. Before I knew it, my elbow was out of the water with my son in my hand. One of the fishing buddies grabbed my son and set him on the bench on the dock. After my son was safe, I pulled myself out of the water and onto the dock. My son was not hurt, but he was shaken up. I haven't really told anyone about this incident, partially because I thought people would attempt to diminish the experience by saying it was caused by adrenaline. I know it was more than that. This all happened within a minute or so, but I know that between the super bright light that lit up the silhouette of my son's body, and what I call a huge hand that got under my feet and thrust me and my son to the dock, this occurrence was nothing short of a miracle.

Turquoise Dress

Several years went by, and I had done some extreme personal work to this point, but was ready for some closure to the underlying pain that still weighed on me. I experienced another sign from above that reaffirmed to me that peace was growing within me, this one taking place in 2005. A month prior to this experience, I received an urgent message from my father in New Hampshire. I knew it was serious because he never called me, as my mother was always the one to reach out.

Living in Seattle at the time, I called Butch back and asked him if everything was OK? Butch, being a man of few words said "your mother was attacked by a German Shepherd and is in the ICU unit in a New Hampshire hospital". I immediately spiraled into desperate questioning about who, what, where, and everything else. My father was able to summarize the event in a straight-forward fashion. My mother was visiting a neighbor across the street from the trailer home they lived in, and the neighbor's huge, black German Shepherd got off its leash and attacked her. The dog ripped my mother's arm up and also bit her in the neck.

Butch said that she had sustained extreme injuries, which was further compounded by the fact that the dog hadn't gotten its rabies shots in years. On top of that, my mother's immune system was weak for a variety of reasons. She had cirrhosis of the liver in the third or fourth stage to accompany her long-standing Crohn's disease. Being over 60 years old with this impaired immune system meant that my mom was ill-equipped for a battle with physical trauma and severe infection.

Still on the phone with Butch, I asked him if I should fly back to New Hampshire to be with her. He told me there was nothing that I could do at this point. He explained that she was in so much pain from the dog attack and infection that she could barely recognize anybody. I was overwhelmed with emotions, but heeded Butch's advice and decided to just check in every day over the phone.

There was one point, about a week later, that my father told me that my mom was semi-alert and was able to recognize him. He said that she asked how her cats and dogs were at home as she wanted to make sure that they were being cared for. Butch also mentioned a really bizarre request from her. She requested that if she were to die, she wanted to wear her favorite turquoise dress at her funeral. This dress was her go-to for her entire life. I must admit that the dress did suit her well. Butch told me that he immediately went home and got that dress out of the closet, just in case.

Sure enough, the infection took hold of her body soon after. About a week later, she took her final deep, gasping breath in front of Butch at the hospital. I flew out the next week to help Butch take care of the funeral arrangements. The funeral was small, comprised of about ten family members. We all were sitting in two rows facing each other, totally speechless. It occurred to me that someone would have to break the silence eventually, being that everyone was in shock that Ma was laying there in the open casket with her turquoise dress on. So I spoke up and said "Isn't it ironic that the very thing that Ma loved the most was what killed her." That was the straw that broke the camel's back, as everyone allowed their repressed emotions to freely flow. All in attendance shared in the moment of grief as the tears were shed. Everyone knew how much she loved her dogs and cats, as well as animals in general. After this moment, the funeral processions were kicked into gear, with each person taking some time to share a few kind words. It was a peaceful and loving end to what had been a hectic and tumultuous life.

Around six months later, I was participating in a sweat lodge, which is a spiritual cleansing process. I had made it through the numerous stages, and was working on finishing up the last phase of the sweat lodge. My duty was the "door man". This job is vital because you bring in the hot river rocks called "Grandfathers" from the fire into the lodge. The other function was to let participants in and out if it became necessary for safety reasons. The leader of the sweat lodge, "The Water Pourer", was facilitating the last process before the sweat was complete. I was the only one outside the sweat lodge and was looking down the wooded hill that lead to the Puget Sound.

At the bottom of the trail, a figure materialized out of the mist. Its form appeared to be feminine and was furnished with a dark head of hair. As the figure walked along the wooded path up the hill, I rubbed my eyes in an attempt to justify this vision with reality. As my eyes readjusted, a new detail about the image became clear: it was wearing a turquoise dress.

It is important to keep in mind that I had just spent over two hours in a very hot spiritual place where I was sweating profusely. Anyway, my fascination compelled me to stay where I was and observe this phenomenon. So I stood there naked in the middle of the woods looking at this mystical figure coming towards me, and eventually it hit me that what I was seeing was my mother. She had her favorite dress on that she wore at her funeral. I found myself completely fixated on her as she slowly moved closer to me. When she got close enough, I noticed that she had a peaceful look of contentment on her face. Although no words were spoken, I received the message that she was in a pain-free state of serenity. At that moment, I felt a warm sensation wash through my body and I started to bawl uncontrollably. Once the tears began flowing, my mother faded away into the mist. The entire encounter couldn't have lasted for more than a minute, but it felt like it took hours for my mom to walk up that path.

As soon as my mother dematerialized back into her etheric realm, I snapped back to reality when I heard the sweat lodge leader say "Door man, open the door!". This is a common command, but it's possible that I didn't hear the initial request. I opened the door and the participants slowly filed out and gathered by the fire outside the lodge. Almost all of the participants were in a highly emotional/spiritual state themselves, so it didn't faze anybody that I was a big pile of mush with a constant river of tears flowing down my face. This was yet another example of me receiving spiritual guidance through physical manifestation.

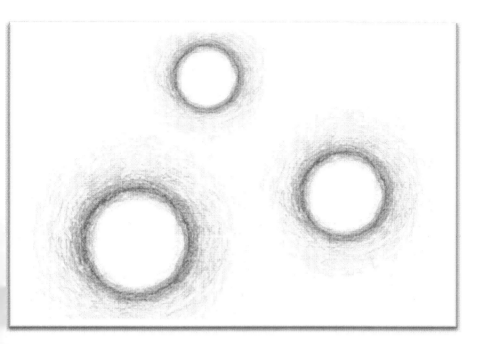

Orbs

My most recent etheric entanglement was in 2017. It was a sunny Saturday afternoon and I had just gotten off work. The day strayed from the norm when I had the sudden urge to take a shower in the afternoon. This was something I almost never did, as I have a long established habit of showering at night before going to bed. But on this day, I decided to deviate from my routine.

Since it was day time, I left the light off in the bathroom. There were two windows in this particular bathroom, but at the time there was no direct sunlight coming through the blinds. I allowed the water to warm up a little bit as I disrobed. When I went to step into the shower, I immediately sensed a presence that was already occupying the shower. It was a strange feeling, but not one that was foreign to me. At this point I was no stranger to moments of spiritual revelation, so instead of feeling nervous I was open to whatever was going to come.

I knew in my heart that something was going to happen so I just stood under the shower head and let the warm water sooth my body. At this moment, my gut told me to close my eyes and pray. So for the next minute or so, I did just that. As my eyes were closed I felt a sensation of heat within my body that was being produced internally and radiating outward. The energy was so unique that it was easily distinguishable from the shower. After taking the time to align with the frequency of whatever was happening, I opened my eyes and was finally able to identify the cause of this occurrence. Circling my head were three glowing orbs. One was an elegant purple, one was bright white, and one was pure gold. These mesmerizing spheres put me into a momentary trance, and I stayed perfectly still while these orbs blessed me in the midst of their orbit. After about 30 seconds, the orbs slowly faded away into the shower mist. I stood in the shower crying tears of joy and peace.

So as I sat in my living room chair, next to the window looking out into my front yard writing about these magical orbs, several light thuds hit my window. I stopped writing to see what was creating the commotion. I noticed about 20 tiny chickadees had landed on the lattice next to my window. A few of the tiny birds had crashed into my window, seemingly in an attempt to get my attention. I sit in this chair every morning and have never seen anything like this before. To me, it was yet another sign that I was supposed to be writing this book to tell my story to others who are hurting. Now that the chickadees are gone I can finish my thoughts.

After doing some research and inquiry into the symbolism of these orbs and their colors, I gained insight into their specific meaning. This particular blessing had come in the form of these angelic orbs, and they were messengers of divine information. The purple orb means to have mercy and transformation. This connected with me on a deep level, as I often allowed my anger and wrath to control me at the expense of others. I had a lethal combination of extreme trauma and military training, and I needed to better corral my built up hostility and be merciful, for my own sake. Only this would lead to the transformation that was also encoded in this purple orb.

The white orb stands for purity and the harmony of holiness. In my view, this represented the fact that I, like every single one of us, has purity as the foundation of our heart. While we may accumulate spiritual grossness that cause impurities and imperfections in our hearts, we are capable of restoring our purity through the pursuit of holiness.

The golden orb represents unconditional love. Much like the sun, which sends us unwavering energy for life, our love for each other needs to be unconditional. My parents put me through what seemed like hell growing up, but at the end of the day they are still my parents and deserve undying love. Our love for one another can be built on this same principal, as our caring actions and feelings should be unassociated with the anticipation of reciprocations. At the time of this experience with the orbs, these were the exact messages that I needed to be presented to me. Although I looked up the meaning of these colors to comprehend them mentally, I had already internalized their meaning in my heart well before my brain could explain it. This power of intuition and feeling lays dormant in many of us in this society that focuses heavily on mental acuity.

For the rest of the week, I felt like a big pile of mush. The paradigm shift was draining, and I knew a lot of hard work was ahead of me. However, each one of these spiritual events strengthens me and provides the necessary energy to continue on the path. I still can't explain why it keeps happening to me, and I may be fortunate to have these experiences, but I firmly believe that we all can feel these things if we keep our hearts and minds open to them. It only takes one to change your life.

Epilogue

In my life's journey, I have been fortunate enough to touch the lives of thousands of people both young and old. My path has been blessed physically, emotionally, intellectually and spiritually. Every step along the pathway of my childhood and beyond, I always felt that something or someone was watching over me. I was supported by many great mentors and friends that knew what I was going through at home as a child. These people loved me and pushed me to work hard in basketball knowing that it was the only positive thing in my life that gave me hope. As you witnessed in your reading, my emotional balance as a young person was put in a blender and stirred into a festering mass of anger. I believe that my only emotional release to defend my inner anger bomb was complete fatigue through athletics and physical exertion to the point of total exhaustion. The pain that I acquired through this exercise was very dysfunctional, but served as a short-term remedy for dealing with my daily dose of drunken parental shenanigans. I am not sure how I made it through all of the physical strain that I put my body through as a child, teenager, and even a young man in the Army. I question the purely physical possibility of how my organs and musculoskeletal system didn't tap out and call it quits during the onslaught of abuse. This leads me to believe that spiritually, a higher power had to be looking over me along my journey and providing me with physical assistance.

During my early days as a child, because I was constantly being led down different paths of destruction, I often doubted there was a God. I realize now that I was blind to the signs that were around me when I was at war as a child. It wasn't until I got out of the Army and started to do some deep, dark personal work on myself that I began to open my eyes and see the signs of spiritual light. It is easy for all of us to get caught up in the drama of everyday life. I still deal with this myself. However, this causes us to miss the little spiritual miracles around us that help us feel the warmth of the higher power. We must all open our eyes and not dismiss the energy around us. I have been blessed with the several holy experiences post-childhood that washed me, and finally helped me see and believe that there truly was something higher in the proverbial clouds. This leads me to believe that I have been spared so I can pass on my story to others that are having hardships and are looking and desperately grasping for hope. For the fortunate ones who had more stable upbringings, I hope your reading of this memoir will leave you feeling fortunate that you weren't scarred as I was. Just maybe in your life journey, you can shape the wisdom from my story to help and support someone who was mentally wounded and in need of some loving guidance.

Postscript

I am glad to report that I now have a great relationship with my father. We have reconciled with each other through forgiveness, which has been a huge emotional blessing for both of us. Although we live on opposite ends of the country, we have still managed to talk every week for the past 15 years. It is refreshing to be able to look back on our rocky path with gratitude, and even laugh at how crazy it all was. Viewing our miseries as blessings has helped us forge a bond that can never be broken.

Made in the USA
Coppell, TX
19 August 2021